Care of the Wild

Care of the Wild

Family First Aid for All Wild Creatures

W. J. JORDAN AND
JOHN HUGHES

RAWSON ASSOCIATES
New York

Library of Congress Cataloging in Publication Data

Jordan, W. J.
  Care of the wild.

  Includes index.
  1. Wildlife rescue. I. Hughes, John, 1930-
II. Title.
QL83.2.J67   1983   636.089   83-3090
ISBN 0-89256-226-9
ISBN 0-89256-240-4 (pbk.)

Composition by
Westchester Book Composition Inc.
Yorktown Heights, New York
Manufactured by
Fairfield Graphics
Fairfield, Pennsylvania
Designed by Jacques Chazaud

First American Edition
English edition published by
Macdonald & Co. (Publishers) Ltd.

Contents

PART THREE: OTHER WILDLIFE

APPENDICES

Acknowledgments

The authors would like to thank the following for help and advice with various aspects of this book.

Donald H. Bliss, Ph.D., M.S.
Agricultural and Veterinary Parasitology Consultant

Daniel O. Farrington, D.V.M., Ph.D.
Former Professor Iowa State Veterinary College.
Director of Developmental Research, Pfizer, Inc.

Samuel Librandi
Fish and Wildlife Service, New York

Christine Stevens
President of Animal Welfare Institute, Washington, D.C.

Before You Begin This Book

Wildlife is everywhere. It abounds in urban areas as well as the countryside: the soil itself teems with life that is essential to our survival, for worms and a million other creatures break down dead material, making nutrients available to new plants; insects provide nutrition for many birds; every bank, roadside, wood, field and garden will be home for some species of rodent which in turn is prey for foxes and other carnivores. Nature does indeed seem to be a random and cruel business, but as we discover more, the picture changes, and we realize there is an all-over design. We know that a rabbit caught by a weasel can die in seconds from shock. We know that morphinelike substances are produced by the nervous system of both humans and animals which reduce pain in certain circumstances. We know that through natural selection prey species become adapted to being preyed on so that if they escape, they soon recover and resume their normal behavior (if they did not, they would suffer from excessive stress, lose weight and die).

But humans, on the other hand, either deliberately or accidentally, inflict injuries to which wildlife is not adapted, and so wildlife suffers. Wild creatures are killed and injured by humans in large numbers: Accidentally many are run over by cars, are poisoned by pesticides or contaminated by oil, and many suffer, intentionally, through shooting, hunting, trapping and poisoning.

You may accidentally strike a bird with the car. It drops to the ground, feathers awry, beak open, eyes closed, but it is still breathing. What do you do? Treat it for shock—but how? Take it to some animal hospital—but where? Should it be put to sleep to end its suffering? How can you make that judgment?

People often come across sick and injured animals and wonder what happens to them. Many have an urge to help but are frustrated by lack of knowledge, and this is why we have written this book.

It may not appear to be suffering, but a bird or mammal that allows itself to be picked up is in serious trouble. Wild creatures are afraid of a person only when he or she comes within their flight line or distance—the distance from a human at which an animal feels safe. A fox or a bird will be calm and inquisitive in the presence of a person, provided he or she is outside the flight distance. It is

ix

important to know that wild creatures often disguise their illnesses and can behave apparently normally until their condition is too serious. Therefore, a good Samaritan should not expect to get more than 20 percent recoveries, a seemingly sad success rate. However, the joy and sense of achievement resulting from the few successes make the trouble worthwhile.

One of the major problems in embarking on care and treatment of a wild animal is that the vast majority do not take kindly to being cared for or treated. Attempting to remove a thorn from a lion's paw is more likely to result in your having your head bitten off than to eternal loyalty from a grateful animal. Lesson number one, therefore, is never to expect gratitude or even cooperation from your patient. This being so, before you attempt to treat the injuries of a wild animal, it is well to know just what injuries you yourself might sustain in the process. Because animals do not react uniformly, it is necessary to consult the appropriate chapter, although there are some general points which apply to all.

In the case of birds, one general piece of advice cannot be overemphasized: No bird should ever be held near the handler's face. There is considerable danger to the eyes in ignoring this simple rule.

Regarding apparent orphans: Do not be in too much of a hurry to take these into your care. If you can assume there is reasonable security from predators, it is far better to leave an apparently healthy young bird where it is found. There is every possibility the parents will continue to feed the infant, and they will make a much better job of it than the finder is likely to do. Similarly, the finding of a very young deer all alone is not sufficient reason in itself for carting it home. It is normal behavior for a mother so to leave an infant. The rearing of any young wild creature is very time- (and patience-) consuming and is fraught with other problems. It should never be lightly undertaken.

It is by no means unusual for a wild patient to "adopt" one human, refusing to have anything to do with anyone else, and it is also helpful in soothing an animal's apprehension if the person attending it presents the same appearance whenever doing so (wearing similar or even identical clothing). As a good example of both these points, John was adopted by a gannet, which could not move and had to be hand-fed while propped up in a large egg box. He was, at that time, a very heavy pipe smoker, and the pipe never left his mouth except when he was eating or sleeping. The gannet, after much initial patience, accepted food readily for several days, then suddenly one day shied away and flatly refused to do so. It took John some time to realize that he was not "wearing" his pipe, which, so far as the gannet was concerned, formed part of John's face. As soon as the pipe was reinserted, food was once again accepted!

Sometimes an animal will accept a woman and not a man (and vice versa). In such cases, it will usually be found that the animal prefers an attendant who is the opposite sex to itself, but there is insufficient evidence to present this as a general principle. A further tip (which would, at one time, have been directed at women only but which these days applies equally to men) is to avoid wearing perfume. This can prove offensive to the sensitive nostrils of many animals, thereby placing the wearer at an initial and quite unnecessary disadvantage in dealing with them.

When you approach a wild animal, a useful point to bear in mind is that eyes which look directly forward, as human eyes do, are generally recognized in nature as the mark of the predator and as such are likely to cause fear and panic. Try to cultivate the habit of not looking directly at an animal. It will not quell the innate fear, but it will almost certainly lessen it.

We would strongly recommend a course of antitetanus injections as being a reasonable and sensible precaution to take for anyone exposing himself or herself to the possibility of being bitten. The possibililty of contracting rabies should never be underestimated in handling any warm-blooded mammal in the United States. If in doubt with any animal, seek expert advice and do not handle it yourself. There are a number of references to rabies in various chapters where appropriate.

We have tried to give hints on what wild animals *can* be fed for limited periods as well as what they *should* be given if kept for prolonged periods. You cannot, after all, have on hand the correct food for any species which might come your way, and you can be sure the casualty will arrive just before a weekend or a public holiday when you can't get what you need.

The primary intention of giving aid and treatment to an injured, diseased or abandoned wild creature is to enable it to return—in health and successfully—to the wild. The animal must not be treated like a pet, for some wild creatures will adapt to humans after their initial fears have subsided. A lack of fear, or a reliance on feeding by humans, or a tendency in some to imprint on, or adopt, a human may lead to disaster if they are then returned to their natural wild state. Every possible care must be taken, therefore, to ensure that while you care for wild and injured creatures, you allow them to maintain a healthy mistrust for human contact so far as possible by no unnecessary handling or even looking.

We have written this book to show you how to help these hurt or orphaned creatures. It will give you simple, down-to-earth information about what to do when you find a wildlife casualty, from how to handle and give first aid to how to doctor, feed and house each creature on its journey back to health.

To give detailed information on every species in the whole of the United States would be beyond the scope of a single volume and the knowledge of anyone. What we are offering is sound basic grounding on what to do for the most common species you are likely to encounter in trouble.

And just who is this "we," and what are our credentials?

W. J. ("Bill") Jordan is a veterinarian with both an impressive list of academic qualifications and a great deal of practical experience.

For sixteen years Bill was in private practice and served as veterinarian to one of the largest zoos in Britain. Following that he spent six years in Iran, where he was consultant clinician to the Iranian government, working with its wildlife. In addition, he looked after the animals belonging to the shah and the royal family. From Iran he went to Africa for two years to lecture at Pretoria University in South Africa and work in the game parks.

Jordan spent the next eight years with the RSPCA, where he formed the society's Wildlife Department and became its first chief wildlife officer, working internationally with such varied species as otters, harp seals, whales and other marine mammals, badgers and tortoises. His current post is director of the People's Trust for Endangered Species.

John Hughes has had a keen interest in wildlife from early childhood. For the past twenty-six years he has been actively engaged in the care and rehabilitation of all manner of wildlife casualties, handling just about every kind of injury wild creatures can suffer, plus rearing many orphans. Hughes probably has more experience in this field than anyone else in Britain.

One field in which Hughes has no peer is in the care, cleaning and rehabilitation of birds contaminated with oil. Experts visit him from all over the world to study his methods and seek advice.

As warden of the RSPCA Wildlife Field Unit he is responsible for wildlife casualties from anywhere in the U.K. He also appears frequently on radio and television, lectures (mainly to natural history societies and the like) and has written two previous books, *The Animals Came In* and *A Monkey About the Place*.

PART ONE

BIRDS

1

Wildfowl (or Waterfowl)

Mute swan

These birds are quite familiar and easily recognizable to most people inasmuch as many live in close proximity to human habitation. They include swans, geese and ducks, and apart from the pointed beaks of the mergansers all have flat or flattish beaks with rounded ends, short legs and webbed feet.

The most widespread of the group is undoubtedly the mallard duck, and there can be few stretches of water anywhere lacking representatives of this species, together with sundry hybrids. The mute swan, too, is widely known, living in a semidomesticated state in many city parks and the like. This is probably why these two species form the bulk of casualties in the group.

Possible Handling Hazards

Most people display a distinct lack of enthusiasm about handling a swan. Once the police phoned us to say a swan had landed right in the middle of a busy road junction and would we please come and remove same, as it was causing a bit of a traffic problem. On arrival at the scene we found the swan had decided to set off—walking—down one of the roads which led to the river about a quarter of a mile distant. Crawling along behind at swan's pace was a police car with flashing light, and behind that was a policeman, directing the traffic clear of the procession! Here were men who would tackle the largest thugs—but tackle a swan? "Not on your life!" one of them emphatically stated.

Biting is no real problem with this group. Although some do try to bite, there is no danger from the beak other than a slight bruising on a fleshy part. Geese have a somewhat stronger nip than the others, but this is still nothing to worry unduly about. Swans seldom try to bite, as though they were aware of their shortcomings in this respect. The *wings* are this group's principal

2

weapons, and these can be wielded to some effect, if not quite to the effect some gory tales would have us believe. It is remotely conceivable that a blow from a swan's wing could break an arm, although we know of no actual cases. It can certainly remove the skin from an unwary shin and be very painful indeed if it happens to catch you in a vulnerable spot. Even a rap from the wing of a duck can be quite painful across the knuckles. A duck will normally use its wings only in defense of a nest or young, whereas a swan or goose will also use them in an attempt to prevent capture.

Approach and Capture

Trying to catch a waterbird on the water is a thankless task, leading to frayed tempers and much derision from onlookers. Best try to avoid it if you can unless you are properly equipped for the job. In general, it will save a great deal of stress and energy (on both sides) if you wait until the bird comes ashore, as it must do from time to time; then try to get between bird and water. Chasing must be kept to the absolute minimum necessary, and a bird will almost certainly flee if approached head-on, no matter how slowly you try. The approach should be made walking slowly *sideways*, and try to avoid looking directly at the bird. In this way it is possible to get close enough to make a final quick move. In the case of a duck, a coat can be thrown over it if no catching net is at hand (a simple catching net can easily be improvised, see fig. 1). In the case of a swan or goose, the aim must be to secure the wings in their folded position, before they can become weapons.

A swan or goose very often will make a great show of belligerence with much hissing and spread wings, in which case you need a bold, direct approach, which usually will cause the bird to turn and run. This is the time to effect a capture, and once the bird has been secured, with wings folded, there is no further danger except for a not uncommon squirt of feces which may catch the catcher!

Note: In defense of a nest or young, a swan or goose will almost invariably stand its ground and put up a fight or even launch a unilateral attack, in spite of any injury it may be suffering.

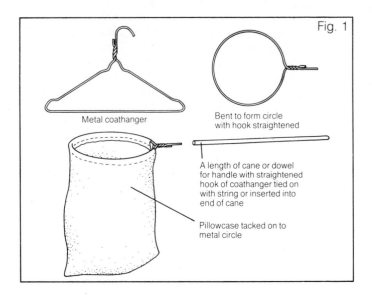

Fig. 1

Metal coathanger

Bent to form circle
with hook straightened

A length of cane or dowel
for handle with straightened
hook of coathanger tied on
with string or inserted into
end of cane

Pillowcase tacked on to
metal circle

Transportation

A duck can be carried in virtually any container large
enough to hold it comfortably so long as air holes are
provided. Should the container be required for use afterward, a generous lining of newspaper or old cloth
will guard against the excess of feces likely to be passed
on the journey. The simplest way to transport a goose
or swan is in a hessian sack (see fig. 2). The bird will
readily poke its head and neck through this hole, and
the open end of the sack can be tied with a piece of
string at the bird's tail end. For a short journey, in the
absence of a sack, the bird can be hobbled with a piece
of thick string or even a handkerchief by bringing the
legs over the folded wings and tying them loosely together (see fig. 3). No matter how quiet it may seem —
and most birds will ride quite quietly without moving
once a vehicle is in motion — do not attempt to carry
the bird loose unless it is screened in some way from
the driver or a second person is holding it. A swan
attempting to fly is not the ideal passenger in heavy
traffic!

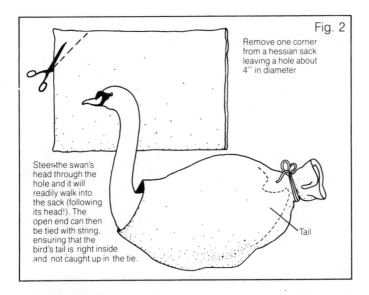

Fig. 2

Remove one corner
from a hessian sack
leaving a hole about
4" in diameter

Steer the swan's
head through the
hole and it will
readily walk into
the sack (following
its head!). The
open end can then
be tied with string,
ensuring that the
bird's tail is right inside
and not caught up in the tie.

Tail

Initial Care

Whatever the reason for bringing in the bird, it is
desirable to provide a quiet room or pen, if possible
warmed to about 68° F (20° C), for at lease the first
twenty-four hours. Cover the floor with wood shavings
or sawdust, if you can find any, or thick newspaper, if
you can't. If you use newspaper, it will need changing
very frequently—you'll be amazed just how much feces
the average swan will deposit, and even a duck can
perform well in this respect. Hay and straw should be
avoided because they may contribute to respiratory problems in a debilitated bird. Food and drinking water
should be provided from the start, for although waterfowl can go without food for several days, your casualty
may already have done so before being found.

Food

Some ducks eat only shellfish, crustaceans and the like,
and most of the group are partial to the odd insect etc.,
though they can fare perfectly well on a vegetarian diet
for the period they are in care. Unless you know the
preference of your patient, it is best at the outset to
provide both types of food since all of them are likely
to eat a little fish if offered. Canned fish (in tomato

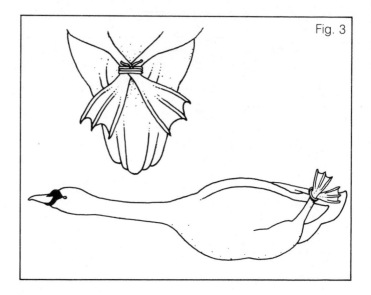

Fig. 3

sauce, not oil) will usually be accepted, as will chopped-up smelt, herring, cod or other whitefish, offered very moist and placed near the main drinking bowl. Canned meat or fish pet food appeal to them, too.

Grass or cabbage (chopped fine) and cornflakes (soaked in water, *not* milk) will be accepted by swans, geese and most ducks. As with the fish, any food offered should be placed immediately adjacent to the main water bowl because they like to "dabble" their food (even their best friends could only describe them as very messy eaters!). The grass or cabbage can be floated on the surface of the main water bowl, and a little bread added. Most lake and river dwellers recognize bread thrown to them by well-wishers as edible, and it will usually tempt them to start feeding, even in the strangest surroundings. Dog biscuits (softened in warm water) are a good wholesome item to offer if it is available, and for the longer term, chick pellets (preferably starter or grower size) and/or mixed corn should be obtained from an animal feed dealer (look in the Yellow Pages if you don't know where there is one). If corn is used, it should be well soaked before feeding. We prefer to use pellets because if the bird is not eating well but is drinking, they can be dissolved in the water and the bird can drink the re-

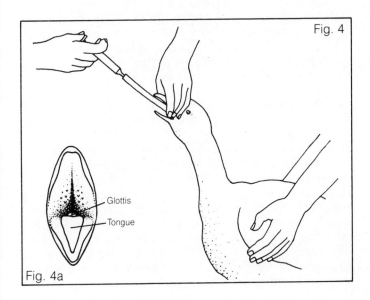

Fig. 4

Glottis

Tongue

Fig. 4a

sultant soup. The mixture looks disgusting but is very nourishing. Float a few pieces of bread on the surface to start with.

Force-feeding

It is unusual for one of this group to refuse all offers, but should this happen and the patient fail to take anything for a two-day period, and there is no obvious obstruction, force-feeding should be attempted pending a possible diagnosis of the trouble. Do not leave it any longer since, as already mentioned, the bird may have eaten nothing for some time prior to capture. Force-feeding is quite a simple operation, the requirements for which are a piece of flexible rubber or plastic tubing roughly the length of a bird's neck and a syringe. The tubing can be up to about three-eighths inch outside diameter. A baby cereal, fish purée or a mixture of both should be used, depending on the patient's species, which should by this time have been established. If still in doubt, use the fish purée.

It is simplest if there are two of you. One holds the bird in a sitting position with neck extended, while the other opens the beak (gentle pressure on the hinge will usually achieve this) and inserts the tube, slightly to one side to avoid the glottis (this is the entrance to the lungs which is situated at the back of the tongue and can easily be seen opening and closing when the beak is open). The tube can be eased gently down the throat, leaving the end protruding for attachment of the syringe (see figs. 4 and 5). *Be sure to hold onto the end of the tube to ensure the bird doesn't swallow it.* If you don't have and cannot get a suitable syringe, an empty liquid detergent bottle can be employed, although it is much more difficult to control.

The mixture should be the thickest that will pass through the syringe, and the quantity should range from a pint per day (divided into three feeds) for a swan down to a quarter of this amount for a small duck such as a teal. The method of administration is simply to keep filling the syringe, attaching it to the tube and slowly and steadily squirting it down. You won't do the bird any harm, provided you don't try to give it too much too quickly (evidence of this would be some of the mixture coming back up again).

Symptoms, Diagnosis and Treatment
Injuries. The most common injuries are caused by fishing tackle and gunshot. Occasionally a bird may break a wing on an overhead wire. More commonly legs get broken.

Swans seem to be particularly susceptible to injuries caused by fishing tackle. Not only does the line become wrapped around the leg, but not infrequently the birds ingest the hook with the line attached—perhaps because of the bait. Sometimes weights are also ingested. Many instances have been recorded. One group that was looking for and recording discarded fishing tackle on a village pond and a reservoir of twenty-two acres for a nine-month period found fifty-two birds and one squirrel entangled with line. Another group over a period of a year dealt with seventy-one birds from thirteen species.

It is possible that discarded tackle may have become more frequent since the introduction of nylon line because an ultrafine size that is almost invisible was produced. It is more likely to break when entangled on branches, weeds, etc. and is more slowly biodegradable because it is impervious to the effects of water or bacteria. Prior to the use of nylon, silk, which decayed fairly rapidly, was used.

Treatment consists of catching the bird and carefully removing the line and hook. If the hook has been swallowed, an operation may be necessary to remove it, and this must be left to a veterinarian. Depending on where it has lodged, it may not cause any symptoms. In this case leave well enough alone for the hook may become encapsulated (grown around with tissue) or may disintegrate.

Postmortem examinations of waterbirds have shown that a considerable number have suffered pellet wounds and recovered. It is unlikely that you will find a bird with superficial pellet wounds unless they are freshly inflicted and the animal is suffering from shock. More usually the bird flies away, and either it recovers or the wounds suppurate and it dies days or weeks later. Pellets pierce the skin and usually travel some distance from the site of entry; it is often best simply to treat the wound with antiseptic and antibiotic and leave it open to drain. If the pellets are lodged in the wing, however, they may be located by shining a bright flashlight through the wing from the underside. This shows up the pellet as a dark opaque spot which, as said before, may be some distance from the entry wound. In these cases it may be useful to probe and squeeze until, with the minimum amount of damage to tissue, the pellet can be extracted.

Wounds close to legs or wings, where the skin is moving, may allow the entry of air, which can travel considerable distances underneath the skin and give it a crackling feel. Try to press this air out gently through the wound, though it is not important to remove it all. Eventually it will be absorbed and disappear as the bird recovers. Large gashes in the skin, especially if near mobile parts, where the healing would be difficult because of continual movement, may be sewn or sutured with a needle and thread that have been sterilized by boiling. Simply pass the needle and thread through the edge of the skin (about one-eighth inch from the edge) and out through the other flap. Cut the thread, pull both ends gently together until the edges of the skin are touching and then tie the thread securely. Place the individual sutures about one-fourth inch or less apart. Always leave an opening at the bottom of the wound so that it will drain. Treatment with antibiotic powder or ointment and bathing with antiseptic solutions are recommended. Birds are more resistant to wound infections than mammals are; nevertheless, it is always advisable to take care.

Old open wounds may be treated by being bathed with antiseptic solutions and applying antibiotic powder or ointment if available. The main essential in treating old wounds is to allow adequate drainage and prevent infestation with maggots. This is usually done by the use of antiseptics that contain phenol or phenol types of compounds.

A broken wing is fairly obvious, for when the bird is at rest, it has an asymmetrical appearance. The wing is not tucked neatly along the body but droops slightly, perhaps sticking out from the general line of the body. If the bird is chased and it opens its wings, the injured wing may droop a little or even trail on the ground. On closer examination, when the wing is pulled out, the bird will attempt to withdraw it, and part will bend at an abnormal angle. Usually the break is halfway along the wing, near what we may call the point or elbow of the wing, for this is the most vulnerable part. The best form of treatment is to bind the broken wing in the normal position to the body of the bird, using elastic strip bandage, leaving the uninjured wing free. More often than not, although healing occurs within two to three weeks, there is less mobility in the mended bone, which may prevent the bird, especially of the larger species, from flying. But usually large birds survive quite well; smaller birds may be in a little more danger from predators.

A broken joint invariably heals by becoming ankylosed—becoming stiff and immobile, rendering the bird unable to fly.

A broken leg is fairly obvious when the bird leaves the water. It is almost completely crippled and will try to hop, using its wings for balance. It is a particularly serious injury in large species like swans, and unless healing returns the leg to near normal, they will be unlikely to survive in the wild. It is essential, therefore, to have the leg splinted as expertly as possible and to keep the bird confined until it has healed, three weeks or so.

The break often occurs in the lower part of the leg, which, being devoid of flesh, is much easier to splint. But if the skin is lacerated, healing may be slow because of the poor blood supply. When the break is high up in the femur, which is surrounded by leg muscles, splinting is very difficult, and the insertion of a steel pin down the shaft of the bone may be possible.

This is done in much the same way as for mammals. The bird is anesthetized, and the skin is incised over the break. The muscles are separated so that the break is exposed. A steel pin of the right thickness and length—that is, not too great for the bony cavity—is pushed into the hollow center of the bone of the longer piece, and the shorter piece is maneuvered over the end. If the break is in the center, it may be necessary to push the pin up the shaft and out through the end, then to position the lower piece and drive the pin down into it. However, there is a danger of causing ankylosis of the joint. This, of course, needs the training, skill and expertise of a veterinarian; indeed, *all* broken wings and legs *should be referred to a veterinarian when possible.*

First-aid splinting of birds in this group requires at least two people—one to hold the bird and the other to apply the splint. A sock pulled over the bird's head will prevent it from seeing, and this will often quiet it considerably. Remember to hold the bird firmly. All handling and manipulations should be firm and delib-

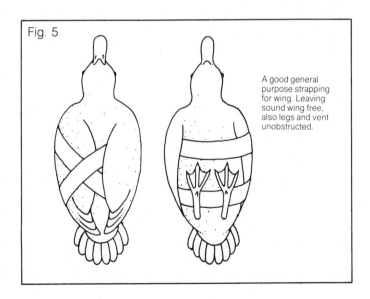

Fig. 5

A good general purpose strapping for wing. Leaving sound wing free, also legs and vent unobstructed.

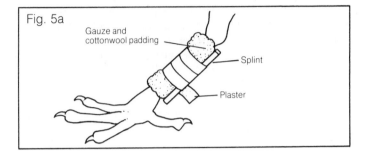

Fig. 5a

Gauze and cottonwool padding

Splint

Plaster

erate; otherwise the bird will struggle at any relaxation of grasp.

Birds have the capacity to feel pain but show less reaction than mammals, so it is not usually necessary to give a general anesthetic—and in any case general anesthetic can be risky in birds. Local anesthetic is usually administered by injection around the affected area. Occasionally in birds the injection may be made around the nerve or nerves supplying the wing or limb, thus blocking all sensation to that part. But birds suffer from shock, which, more often than not, is caused by fear, and tranquilizers are sometimes used.

To splint a wing, simply hold both wings along the body in the normal position, and wind adhesive tape over the broken wing and around the body, leaving the uninjured wing free. To splint a break in the lower part of the leg, first place a small amount of gauze and then absorbent cotton around the limb. Place a splint (a section of split bamboo cut to the correct length to extend from the joint above the break to the joint below) along the leg, and bind it in place with adhesive tape or insulating tape with the leg held stretched in the normal position. For a break in the fleshy part of the leg, it is essential to refer to a veterinary surgeon.

Once the break has healed, remove the bandage or tape by first cutting it into small portions and then carefully peeling it off so as not to damage the feathers.

Diseases and Poisoning. Loss of locomotion is fairly common in this group of birds, and there are many causes—from shock and poisoning to general weakness caused by chronic disease. When you find a bird that seems unable or unwilling to move or can move only very feebly, first feel its breastbone to see what sort of condition it is in. If the bird is plump and its feathers seem to be in good condition, apart from those that may be damaged, the cause is likely to be of recent origin and may be lead poisoning or poisoning from pesticides or insecticides. If, on the other hand, the bird is thin and emaciated and looks bedraggled, it is quite possible that the disease is of longer duration and hope of cure, therefore, is more remote.

Postmortems of mute swans have shown lead poisoning to be a frequent cause of death, and research into such deaths is now in progress. The main cause is thought to be weights from fishing tackle—lead pellets which are split so that they can be clamped on the line. One mute swan was found to have forty-four pieces in its gizzard. The pellets are gradually acted upon by digestive juices, and lead is continuously absorbed. It is a cumulative poison, and as the level in the body rises, the bird begins to pass a greenish offensive-smelling diarrhea. It loses weight, and many birds develop a neck paralysis before general paralysis sets in.

Another source of lead poisoning is in the ingestion of lead shot from cartridges. As it has no split in it, it can be easily distinguished from fishing weights. Fallen shot is abundant in areas where wildfowl are hunted, and it has also caused poisoning in mute swans and waterfowl. The lead pellets lie in the mud and seem to be swallowed as an alternative to stones. They lodge in the gizzard and are gradually worn away, and some are absorbed. This problem of lead poisoning caused by ingestion of lead pellets was first noticed in the United States, and many hunters are now using cartridges that contain stainless steel shot rather than lead, so serious has the poisoning become.

Bill was presented with an interesting case that parallels this problem. An ostrich was suffering from loss of appetite and loss of weight and was passing greenish fetid diarrhea. A clinical examination suggested poisoning—but what? The bird was penned with others that were healthy, but it was possible that a member of the public had given the bird some poison. An exhaustive search plus a bit of inspiration, and it was discovered that a padlock was missing (a new padlock on the gate had been noticed). A metal detector was fetched, and it reacted. The bird was operated upon, and not one but two padlocks were removed. Both had lost most of their galvanized zinc coating.

To return to lead poisoning, lead shot is not the only source found. Lead weights used by fishermen to weight down lines are often lost in the water. The normal-sized pellets will be completely dissolved by the digestive jucies within forty days or so. But absorption doesn't always occur uniformly, and the birds' livers will be able to detoxify some lead. Swans, for example, can remain healthy with up to three or four pellets in their gizzards. Stress can sometimes precipitate symptoms suddenly and can cause rapid death. However, usually the affected birds begin to lose weight, become anemic, and have difficulty feeding. Green diarrhea develops, and the bird begins to show first neck weakness, then feebleness of the wing muscles, and then leg weakness. In other words, the neck is not held in the normal position but kinks and allows the back of the neck to rest on the back of the bird. Then the bird won't or can't fly, and later it begins to stagger. Paralysis soon follows.

Treatment is worthwhile if it is fairly specific. It consists of injecting into the bloodstream a chelating agent such as calcium versonate or calcium edetate (which may do better) and giving a course of d-penicillamine by mouth to stop the uptake of lead. One vet has described how he was able to pass a tube into the gizzard and suck out the remaining pellets. Needless to say, treatment for lead poisoning *can be given only by a veterinarian* because the dose of treatment must be accurately graded to the amount of lead present. And of course, an x-ray will help by showing how many pellets are left in the gizzard. Most birds show an immediate improvement but will soon relapse if treatment is not continued till all the lead has been eliminated.

Good nursing, including tube feeding (see "Force-feeding"), is essential during treatment.

Botulism is a type of poisoning caused by the ingestion of materials containing toxin derived from a bacterium called *Clostridium botulinum*. This flourishes in warm, damp conditions, such as lake edges which are drying out but which still have plenty of damp mud exposed to the warming effects of the sun. The organism grows on rotting vegetation on the borders of the lake under what are called anaerobic conditions (without the presence of oxygen). The toxin is produced and remains viable for a considerable period of time. It is very potent, and only a small amount is necessary to kill a bird by respiratory paralysis. Waterbirds come down and feed on the toxic vegetation and are often found dead in large numbers. A few are found alive, but paralyzed, and may be treated by being given appreciable quantities of water by tubing (see "Force-feeding"). But there is no really effective antidotal treatment, and there is little or nothing to be seen on postmortem examination.

Insecticides are widely used in agriculture and horticulture and are highly toxic to other forms of life such as birds and mammals. Fortunately this group of birds is not often exposed either accidentally or maliciously to this form of poisoning.

Poisoning by excessive feeding of white bread has also been described, though it has not been investigated thoroughly. It is said to cause diarrhea, which will clear up when white bread is replaced by normal food.

Salmonellosis, psittacosis, tuberculosis and pseudotuberculosis all can occur in this group, but only on rare occasions. These diseases, therefore, will be described later in this book in other groups which are more frequently affected.

Gizzard and intestinal worms not infrequently affect this group, geese in particular. They cause loss of condition in spite of normal appetite. They can be diagnosed by a veterinarian from a sample of droppings, and it is quite possible to treat them successfully. However, you are not likely to meet with this problem in a recognizable form unless you are nursing a bird for other reasons and find that it is feeding fairly well yet not putting on weight. When this happens, some thought should be given to the possibility of internal parasites.

Bumblefoot is an abscess on the pads of the feet of birds and is occasionally found in this group. Various bacteria, but most often staphylococcus, are responsible. Treatment consists in opening the hard lump, expressing the pus and treating the inside with iodine solution, and keeping the bird on a hard, dry, clean surface until the wound has totally healed.

Oil Pollution
Wildfowl, as well as sea birds, are frequent victims of oil spillage because no stretch of water is safe from this

hazard. This particular problem is dealt with separately in Chapter 7.

General Care

The plumage of wildfowl is apt to deteriorate if birds are kept indoors for long periods, so provided the treatment will allow it, as soon as possible after the first twenty-four hours the patient should be moved outside, where its plumage can "weather" in the normal way. It is not necessary to provide a house, but a windbreak would be appreciated. If there isn't much rain about, a good spray of clean water from a hose or even a watering can each day will be beneficial, and if it is possible to provide bathing facilities, again if treatment or dressings will allow, so much the better. A grass paddock is preferable because prolonged confinement to a hard surface is likely to lead to foot sores.

Release

Many birds in this group will fly off on their own when ready to do so. It is, for instance, a complete fallacy that a swan needs a long stretch of water in order to get into the air. A healthy bird can take off and clear a six-foot fence with a dry runway of no more than about ten yards.

Leaving in this way is a good indication that the bird is ready to fend for itself once again, but since it isn't always practicable to provide conditions conducive to a free takeoff, you may have to take your ex-patient to a suitable release point. Since some of this group may lose the sharp edge of their natural wariness during a period of captivity, the release point should be as far away from people as possible and inasmuch as some species are territorial (indeed, *most* are when nesting or raising a family), it may be judicious to select a stretch of water free of the bird's own species where it can orient itself without interference.

Orphans

Mallard (male)

Some ducks are inclined to nest some distance away from water. Why do they do this? you may ask. The banks of rivers and lakes are very busy places by day, with people boating, fishing and swimming or simply walking along with big feet likely to step on eggs, perhaps accompanied by bounding dogs likely to cause annoyance to a broody mom; by night, with the odd fox or mink on the lookout for an easy meal. One way or another, it isn't such a bad idea to set up house elsewhere. And then, when the ducklings are hatched, the duck will set off to walk to the water, leading the brood. Besides, the practice does produce the occasional heartwarming picture of someone stopping traffic to allow a duck and her family to cross the road!

Unfortunately it is by no means an unusual occurrence for the duck to disappear during this hazardous journey, probably into someone's oven, since she makes a very easy catch at this time. Thus the ducklings are left milling around aimlessly.

Since they feed themselves from birth, ducklings are comparatively easy to care for if a constant source of warmth can be provided where they sleep and a few other simple rules are observed. *In the following advice the term* ducklings *also applies to cygnets and goslings.*

An infrared lamp, which may be borrowed from a farm or kennel, is by far the best form of heating for nurturing ducklings, but the enclosure must be large enough to permit them to move away from the heat when they wish to do so. In the absence of such a lamp, some other type of safe heating must be improvised to keep the temperature at the sleeping place around 95° to 104° F (35°–40° C). Failing anything else, keep the ducklings in the warmest possible room, and provide in one corner of the enclosure a dry mop head, which the brood can nestle under and around as a mother substitute. A broody hen or bantam, should one be available, will offer excellent services as a foster mother, dispensing with the need for artificial heat.

Although they can be seen swimming quite happily with their mothers in the wild, orphaned ducklings must not be allowed to enter water until they begin to grow feathers, even though they will try their utmost to do so. The down of their early days is simply not waterproof, and they will quickly become saturated. Until recent years it was thought the preen-gland wax of the mother was transferred to the young during brooding each night, thus affording them buoyancy, but we now know that this wax has nothing to do with buoyancy (see Chapter 7). However, there seems no doubt that *some* secretion from the mother is essential in these early days to enable the young to enter the water safely.

Newspapers are not satisfactory as floor covering for

ducklings. They are unable to maintain a firm footing, and this can lead to permanent leg distortions. Sawdust is recommended for most of the enclosure, with a patch of floor left clear for the food. Alternatively, old cloth such as toweling can be used if there are no loose threads which can (and will) become entangled around the ducklings' legs. Paper towels would probably provide a rough enough surface but may prove rather expensive since the floor covering needs to be changed very frequently.

Throughout the period of care, stay away from the ducklings as much as possible so they do not become accustomed to close human presence, and do not handle them any more than absolutely necessary.

Although they cannot be allowed to get into water, the ducklings must be provided with a generous and constant supply for drinking, and the best piece of equipment to provide this is a chick drinking fountain, obtainable from most pet stores or agricultural merchants. If necessary, a fountain can be improvised, using a jam jar and saucer (see fig. 6).

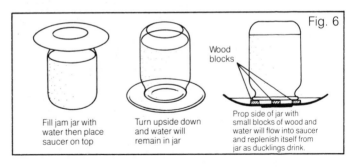

Fig. 6

Wood blocks

Fill jam jar with water then place saucer on top

Turn upside down and water will remain in jar

Prop side of jar with small blocks of wood and water will flow into saucer and replenish itself from jar as ducklings drink.

For food provide all, or as many as possible, of the following each day: fine-chopped hard-boiled egg; fine-chopped grass; chick mash/insectivorous mixture. It is difficult to give a precise guide to quantities, but suffice it to say ducklings will eat a great deal more than you might imagine, so be generous. They will not overeat.

Chick mash can be obtained from an animal feed dealer or possibly a pet store. Small ducklings find mash easier to assimilate than even the smallest pellets, although pellets can be used for cygnets and goslings from the start. Ducklings can move onto starter pellets after about two weeks. Insectivorous mixture can be obtained from any pet store or in bulk from a specialist merchant (for further information, call your nearest zoo). Mix the pellets and insectivorous mixture together in equal proportions and serve dry but, as with all food, adjacent to the drinking fountain. The chopped egg and grass will keep the ducklings going until you are able to get the other items. It is best simply to scatter the food on the floor, clearing away each morning any left over from the previous day. Do not leave stale food around.

If you do not know the species of your ducklings, it would be as well to provide some fish, as mentioned earlier for an adult. Place this in a container low enough for the ducklings to reach into but small enough to preclude their getting in for a bath. The pots in which some sandwich spreads are sold are ideal.

The length of time the heater will be needed will depend on the ambient temperature and the species involved. The best way is to let them decide for themselves. If you pay a quiet visit after they have settled down for the night on two or three occasions and find they have moved their sleeping position well away from the lamp, it is safe to dispense with its use. After about a week without a heater and provided the weather is mild, the ducklings can be transferred to an outside pen with a shelter they can get under in heavy rain (they will, in fact, usually do this). Light showers will do no harm at this stage and will help get rid of the dirt they accumulate because they are denied bathing.

The species in this group do not all get their feathers at the same age, so keep a lookout for feathers appearing. When the breast is covered, the ducklings can be allowed to bathe ad lib. It is not necessary to wait until they are fully fledged (when they have their main wing feathers).

The time for release is when they *are* fully fledged, and as with adult casualties, it is better they make their own decision and fly off when ready. If they must be taken for release, follow the same suggestions as for adult casualty releases and, if possible, provide some of the food they have become accustomed to somewhere in the vicinity for the first few days, even though it is likely to be eaten by every other bird in the area!

2

Other Swimming Birds
(Including Sea Birds)

This chapter covers a pretty wide field, but the physical details common to most in the group are pointed beaks and webbed (or partially webbed) feet. The size ranges from the white pelican at up to six feet and with a wingspan of nine feet to the least tern at about ten inches. Neck length varies from very long to hardly any.

Least tern

The most common in the group, and the most widely encountered, is the herring gull, vast numbers of which now never go near the sea, spending their lives on rubbish dumps, where the pickings are much richer. At the other extreme, many of the group such as the auks (murres, razorbills, etc.) never come anywhere near humans unless some disaster befalls them, such as being covered with oil.

Possible Handling Hazards

All of this group can, and will, bite, and most can draw blood. The severity of the bite, of course, varies enormously. The long powerful beak of the gannet, with an edge serrated like a hacksaw blade, can cause quite a severe laceration to a bare arm, while the much smaller and more delicate kittiwake will give only a minor nip. But do not take the size of the bird as the criterion for the severity of the bite—the efforts of some of the smaller members of the group can be memorable!

Although the claws are not used as weapons, it should be remembered that birds with webbed feet still have claws at the end of them, and these can scratch quite painfully if the bird is handled clumsily. Be prepared, too, for strong vocal protests from the bird.

Approach and Capture

The circumstances in which one of this group might be found in distress are so wide and varied that it is virtually impossible to generalize on approach and capture. The flight line or distance varies considerably and is also affected by the incapacitating factor. In other words, a fit bird might feel quite safe at X feet, but the same bird, if injured, may feel it needs a much greater margin in order to effect an escape and so may well start running (if we assume injury to wing, not leg) before you have even spotted it. Others may opt for trying to hide, and this offers the easiest capturing prospect since most of the group aren't very good at hiding.

As with the previous group, any waterbird feels safer on the water and so will, of course, try to reach this safety when approached. It is imperative that the catcher impose himself between water and bird if he is to have any chance of an effective capture, and once he has done so, a slow, sideways approach, as in Chapter 1, is recommended. Some of the group, such as grebes and loons, are not very good on their feet, whereas gulls, for example, can run very rapidly indeed. It is preferable to enlist the aid of several people to catch a bird rather than have one person drive it to exhaustion.

For those unaccustomed to handling, or if you do not recognize the bird and are unaware of its capacity for doing you a bit of no good when you try to get hold of it, the simple "throw a coat over it" routine is the best option for initial capture unless you are equipped with a catching net (fig. 7). When this has been effected, remove the coat slowly and grasp the bird firmly with one hand just behind the head. With the other hand,

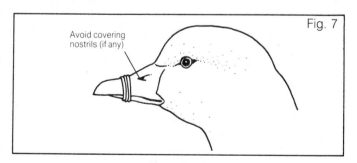

Fig. 7

Avoid covering nostrils (if any)

or the knees if it is a large species, secure the wings from flapping. With an elastic band, a piece of string or, if nothing else is available, the hem torn from a handkerchief or some other piece of cloth, secure the beak, taking care not to cover the nostrils (some species in this group have no apparent nostrils but can still breathe with beak secured).

Do not make the error of feeling completely safe with the beak taped because many of this group can and undoubtedly will stab with the point. So it can do no harm to reiterate the warning: *Do not hold any bird near your face.*

Transportation

Any well-ventilated container can be used for transport, provided it is large enough for the particular bird— i.e., the bird should be able to sit in a natural posture with no distortion of the plumage.

The tape on the beak should be removed for the journey because some birds in this group tend to vomit after being under stress (the chase and capture by a human, for instance). If this vomiting is not observed and the tape quickly removed, there is a great danger of asphyxiation.

As with waterfowl, if the container is required for subsequent service, line it with newspaper or cloth for the journey; otherwise it will be fit only for the garbage can when you reach your destination.

We have had birds transported to us successfully in all manner of containers: shopping bags; duffel bags; even paper bags. But do not make the same mistake as a well-meaning gentleman who traveled sixty miles to bring in a bird he had found on the beach. He had placed it in a drawstring plastic bag, but instead of drawing up the string, leaving the head protruding, he had enclosed the whole bird, and it had suffocated, probably only a short time after he set off on his long journey.

Initial Care

Just as with a human, if a bird is not naturally exposed to infection, it has no opportunity to build up immunity. Sea birds in particular are highly susceptible to an infection of the lung called aspergillosis, so do not house your patient in an old dusty building where the lethal spores might lurk. Hay and straw are also very suspect and should be avoided in any building housing sea birds. Thick newspaper is best for the floor, and there is no need to provide any kind of bed because the bird will simply sleep at any point within the enclosure and not necessarily the same place twice. A period of warmth (about 68° F, 20° C), peace and quiet will be most beneficial initially, with food and drink at hand.

Food

All of this group eat fish, and some will eat nothing else. This can range from whitebait to full-size herring, depending on the size of the patient. The fish should be offered whole, if the appropriate size can be readily obtained, inasmuch as some birds do not appear to recognize strips of fish as being fish. You do not, after all, find many strips of fish swimming about in the sea.

There is no greater connoisseur of fresh fish than a sea bird, so it is useless offering anything which is a little off, but frozen fish (after thawing, of course) will be found acceptable in most cases.

The fish should be offered in a shallow dish with just a little water, sufficient to keep it moist. There is no necessity to offer any other water, salted or otherwise. For a pelican, the fish should be placed in the bill pouch.

Some of the gulls, the herring gull in particular, will accept canned dog or cat food readily. Indeed, a herring gull will eat virtually anything edible, hence the great success of the species, but if the patient is being fed on anything dryer than fish, it is recommended that a bowl of additional water be available. It is not necessary to add salt.

Failing anything else, canned fish (in tomato sauce, not oil) will find favor with most gulls and grebes but are unlikely to tempt the ocean birds such as the auks.

If in doubt about which fish to buy, go for the smallest. A larger bird can eat small fish, but not the other way around, and whitefish or sprats (a small herring) will be found acceptable to most of the group. Some of the larger species such as cormorants will appreciate dead day-old chicks (see Chapter 5).

Murre

Force-feeding

Gannet

If this should prove necessary—and give the patient at least twenty-four hours before considering it—the job is best tackled by two people—in the case of a gannet, three if they are available!

For most of the group, small firm sprats are best to use for the purpose since they are easiest to administer. For the larger species, herring are best.

One person can catch and hold the bird while the other does the actual force-feeding. The holder can wear gloves, but the feeder cannot since it is virtually impossible to open the beaks of most of this group if you wear gloves. So it is up to the holder to save the feeder from being bitten by holding the bird firmly with one hand just behind the head until the feeder has grasped the beak, and the fish should be given head first.

As should be apparent by now, the beaks of most of this group are quite strong with powerful jaw muscles; consequently, many of them are difficult to open. Conversely, once they *are* open, they are comparatively easy to retain so while the fish is popped in and pushed well down the throat (see fig. 8).

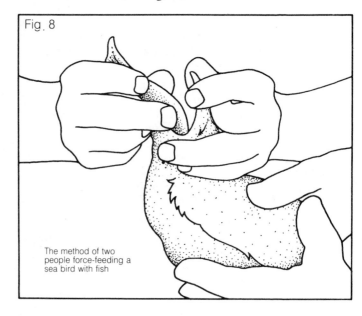

Fig. 8

The method of two people force-feeding a sea bird with fish

It is difficult to know just how many fish to give in force-feeding, and it is equally difficult to lay down set rules, because so much depends on the species of bird being dealt with and the size of the fish. As a general rule, two fish—of a size the bird can comfortably swallow—twice a day should be sufficient to keep the patient going, and of course, additional fish should always be left within reach. These should always be counted so that it can quickly be seen if the patient has taken any voluntarily. As soon as it does so, force-feeding should cease.

Symptoms, Diagnosis and Treatment
Injuries. These are rare in purely sea birds or, at least, do not come to the attention of the public mainly because they spend all of their time at sea or along the coast. However, as already mentioned, some gulls live inland, scavenging among garbage for a living, and other members of the group also live inland. In doing so, they often suffer wing injuries from flying into wires or other objects, and of course, they are shot at by people from time to time and suffer wounds from pellets. It is rare to find a gull with a broken leg.

Treatment of broken wings follows the same pattern as for wildfowl (see pages 10–12). Two people are necessary, and the wing must be held in place while it is bound to the body. With gulls, total success is difficult to achieve. These birds spend so much time in the air—using their wings for gliding as well as flying—and the union of the broken bones has to be exactly right for the bird to be able to fly sufficiently well.

Although many gulls have had broken wings treated, it is often impossible to release them back to the wild, and many are kept for their lifetimes, which are quite long (can be as long as thirty years), in captivity. It is during these long periods that infections such as aspergillosis of the lungs and staphylococcal infection of the legs, occur.

Generally the birds do not feed in areas where botulism poisoning can occur, nor do they pick up lead shot or lead pellets.

Alpha-Chlorolose, a narcotic drug which renders the bird unconscious, is used to capture "nuisance" birds. When the birds eat enough of the drug, they become narcotized and unable to fly. Some lie quietly asleep, while others flap and stagger about in a drunken manner. The birds are semiconscious and not suffering, in the true sense of that word. Nevertheless, it is upsetting to the public, and for this reason, those who lay the bait generally have sufficient personnel available to pick up the narcotized birds as quickly as possible.

Herring gull

Should nontarget birds become affected, it is possible to treat them, if they have not eaten too large a dose, by keeping them warm and giving them fluids when they are alert enough to take them. Provided that the dose is not a lethal one, the bird will gradually recover.

Several other preparations are used for the control of birds, and these are mentioned in this section of Chapter 6.

Oil Pollution
This is by far the most major hazard for sea birds, requiring separate discussion (see Chapter 7).

General Care
A sea bird can be kept away from water (for swimming) for quite some time with no apparent deterioration of the plumage, certainly for the three or four weeks an injury may take to heal. So it isn't strictly necessary to provide a pond (see Chapter 7), although most will enjoy a dip if it can be offered.

When the birds are moved out of doors (always desirable as soon as possible with any patient), a grass paddock or aviary is preferable for the larger members of the group and for the grebes and loons, while a smooth concrete surface is recommended for the auks and gulls.

Release
This should be at the earliest possible moment since some of the group very easily become tame to the point of following a human around like a dog, a condition which will be unlikely to benefit their health when they are released since some vandal will undoubtedly feel obliged to kill such birds. Grebes and loons will quickly soil their plumage if they are unable to get into water.

When ready to do so, the average gull will fly off from anywhere, but others of the group simply cannot orient themselves when out of sight of the sea and will make no attempt to fly, even from an open pen. Most of the group should be taken to the seashore, preferably at some quiet spot, for release; grebes, to any large stretch of water. If the bird is fit, it will normally take to the water or the air immediately, although a gannet or pelican will occasionally stand motionless on the shore for quite some time, thinking about it, before departure.

Orphans

Apart from gulls, the herring gull in particular, *nestlings* of this group seldom, if ever, are likely to be found in circumstances suggesting they might be orphans. The reason is simply that most prefer to nest well away from human habitation, many on quite inaccessible cliff ledges, and should the nest be left unattended for any length of time, the occupants will themselves quickly make a meal for a predator. But very occasionally *fledglings* may be picked up, and they can be cared for in the same manner as an adult bird since they are likely to be quite self-sufficient so far as feeding is concerned.

White pelican

Because many gulls have taken to nesting on buildings, it is by no means unusual for very young chicks to be picked up for various reasons—such as falling down a chimney. Perhaps we have just been fortunate, but the gull chicks we have had have accepted food readily, without resort to elaborate subterfuge. Canned fish in tomato sauce mixed with breadcrumbs generally go down very well, and often canned dog food is happily eaten. The food should be quite wet at first but with plenty of decent-sized lumps the youngster can easily get hold of. A dish of water should be left next to the food bowl, and most chicks will dabble their beaks in this.

The subterfuge mentioned above is based on natural feeding behavior in the nest. Adult gulls have on the underside of their beaks a red spot which the chick will tap and worry at, thereby stimulating the parent to regurgitate the food. An artificial beak is presented to the chick, complete with red spot for it to tap, and it is an established fact that the chick will instinctively do this, no matter how inexpertly the beak has been fashioned. A quantity of food is then deposited for the chick to gobble up.

We have no doubt that this probably does work and would recommend it be tried should you be presented

with a reluctant chick. But, as mentioned above, we
have experienced no such problem; most gull chicks of
our acquaintance have eaten us out of house and home
with absolutely no artificial stimulation!

*Common
loon*

A human-reared gull chick may hang around the
garden for a considerable time but usually will depart
eventually. Some will set off to make their own way in
the world as soon as they are fully fledged. It is always
best to let them make up their own minds, if you have
the room to do so, rather than take them away somewhere strange for release. If they leave under their own
steam, they will be able to find their way back should
they find the pickings lean elsewhere.

A friend who runs a bird hospital offered a bit of
interesting information about the fulmar, which is a
bird very much like the gull in appearance but with
tubular nostrils. It seems that in the latter stages of
fledging, when the youngster very much resembles the
adult in appearance but cannot yet fly, it is fattened up
by the parents, then left on the breeding ledge to complete its feather growth. At this time it is apt to be set
upon by gulls and forced off the ledge. It will then plane
down to the water and float into the beach. It seems
fulmars do not feed during this period, so should you
happen to come across one, there is no point in trying
to feed it. It will live on its own fat until fully fledged,
by which time the wings will protrude beyond the tail,
and it can then be released. If you should be attempting
to keep more than one, they should be kept separately;
otherwise they will squirt an oily fluid at one another
and make an awful mess!

It should be mentioned that there are some casualties
that really aren't casualties at all. Some birds simply
cannot take off from flat ground, the manx shearwater
being a case in point, and from time to time one is
blown inland during a gale and is found apparently
unable to fly. John remembers one occasion when a car
arrived with a party of young men and a shearwater
they'd found some thirty miles away. The spokesman
was most solicitous. "It seems to be injured," he said.
"It was just sort of crawling around on the ground."
Although it was quite apparent (to us) what the problem
was, the bird was given a thorough examination (the
least we could do after they'd come so far), after which

it was pronounced fit and thrown into the air much to the alarm of the anxious onlookers. Their faces were a picture as the bird disappeared into the distance, heading for the coast.

3

Waders (and Similar)

Coot

We have added the *and Similar* since some of the birds in this group are not, strictly speaking, waders. We have, for example, included coots and gallinules not only because of similar physical appearance but because they can also be cared for in a similar way.

The notable feature of the group is long legs with unwebbed feet. Beaks range from short and straight to long and straight and long and curved. All are pointed— with the exception of the spoonbill, which might be encountered on the coast of Texas or Florida, and has a very distinctive beak, as its name implies. Neck length, too, varies from very short to very long. This always reminds us of a certain woman who telephoned to tell us of an injured bird she had encountered, describing it as "a duck with a long neck." The bird turned out to be a bittern!

As with the previous group, there is quite a range of sizes with the great blue heron at one end, measuring around four feet to the tiny piping plover at the other, measuring a mere six inches. From a casualty point of view, the herons are probably the most common, very often coming to grief in collisions with overhead cables. They also suffer badly during hard winters.

Possible Handling Hazards

The greatest danger from this group, particularly the larger of them, is to underestimate the reach of the neck. The bird will frequently make a stab for the handler's eyes if it is given the opportunity, and herons, for example, have a very long reach indeed. All of the group have this distinctive stabbing action of the beak, which is, after all, their method of catching food but which can be disconcerting, to say the least, when you are on the receiving end. However, most of the smaller ones have no defense at all other than to try desperately to escape.

Approach and Capture

Many of this group have a propensity for paddling in boggy, marshy ground which often means the rescuer must flounder about in Wellington boots in order to catch a still-mobile injured bird. Others inhabit more solid beaches but can get up a very respectable turn of speed, with long legs moving so rapidly they can hardly be seen, and since most, if not all, of the group are exceptionally shy and nervous, an approach can be most difficult. Others will simply hide when a human appears, and their camouflage is quite impeccable.

We can offer no easy formula for capture except, as suggested in the previous chapter, to try to enlist the aid of several people. It will cause less stress to the bird in the long run if it can be secured quickly.

It is particularly important with this group to keep the bird well away from the face and never to underestimate the reach. The larger birds should be held with one hand just behind the head, but do be careful not to twist the neck in any way. As a general rule, the bird will remain quite still once it finds itself securely held, but don't be lulled into relaxing the hold behind the head or you may easily lose the sight of an eye. As mentioned earlier, most of the smaller members of this group will attempt no defense at all when captured but will be very distressed at the close proximity to a human. This can be alleviated by removing yourself from the bird's view, and the simplest way of doing this is to place a handkerchief over the bird's head until it is placed in the traveling container.

Transportation

It is desirable, indeed essential in the case of long journeys, that the bird should have enough room to stand up since long-legged birds, particularly the larger ones, can very easily get cramp and even paralysis if the legs are kept artificially folded for any length of time. With the smaller members of the group, this is no great problem since they aren't very tall, but containers of sufficient depth to hold a heron don't come easily to hand. The simplest solution is to tie a handkerchief over the bird's head, leaving the beak free, and to let it travel loose. It is unlikely to move if it cannot see, but if for any reason this course is not practicable or, indeed, if the bird has a broken leg, then it is best to secure the wings to the body, as well as to cover the head, and to lay the bird on its side with the legs stretched out.

The type of container for the small members of this group can be virtually anything of sufficient size to contain the bird in question. Even a paper bag with a few air holes will usually be sufficient to contain a small wader. It will prefer the security of being in hiding rather than make any attempt to escape from the container.

Initial Care

Being offered somewhere to hide will contribute immeasurably to the recovery of any casualty in this group. What this consists of is quite immaterial, just so long as the bird can get out of sight: a screen of any sort, even a small table or stool laid on its side, anything which allows the bird to disappear from view when you approach the room or pen in which it is being housed.

Sawdust is the best floor covering for this group, or cloth if this is not available. Newspaper *can* be used, but some of the group find it too smooth for comfortable walking.

As with all casualties, a period of adjustment in warmth and quiet with food and water available is essential. It is best not to attempt any treatment, unless this should be imperative—to staunch a flow of blood, for instance—until the day after arrival when the bird, it is hoped, will be in a better state to cope with the additional stress involved. But the patient will almost certainly benefit from the immediate administration of some fluid before being left to rest (see "Symptoms, Diagnosis and Treatment" in Chapter 6).

Food

Fish is the best thing to offer any of this group—mashed whitefish or whole sprats (small herrings), depending on the size of the patient (and the size of the fish). Also, for the smaller patients, the more solid types of canned dog food, chopped up and minced, or small strips of raw meat can be given. The large members of the group such as the heron or egret will usually accept sprats and sometimes a dead chick or mouse if one or other is available, but do not give a mouse you just happen to find dead since it may have been poisoned.

Small crustaceans, such as shrimp, will be eaten by some, principally the shore dwellers, and chopped hard-boiled egg may also be accepted by many of the smaller members of the group. Do not be afraid to try *anything* if you think it may stimulate the appetite. If your patient will accept it voluntarily, it is unlikely to cause any harm for a limited period. Failing anything else, we would suspect that many members of this group would accept caviar, if you can afford to try it! Offer fish in a dish or bowl of water, and the other food moist (apart from the chicks, mice and egg), and keep a bowl of clean water in the pen.

A certain amount of experimentation may also be required into *how* the food is presented. Your patient may accept food from a blue dish when it flatly refused the same item from a red one. It may scorn any dish but gobble up the food readily when it is simply scattered on the floor. It may refuse all blandishments when inside a building only to eat like a horse when transferred to an outside pen.

Do not stand around waiting to see the bird eat because it almost certainly won't while you are there. Take careful note of the quantity of anything you give so you are able to ascertain later if any has been consumed. It is always better to offer a choice of several things rather than try them out one at a time. The bird may be dead by the time an acceptable diet is found.

Force-feeding

In general, we do not recommend attempting to force-feed members of this group. For one thing, with the smaller long-beaked species, there is considerable danger of damage to the beak when you attempt to open it and hold it open, but another much more significant reason is the extreme nervousness of this particular group, which usually causes them to vomit immediately afterward anything they have been forced to eat. There seems little point in subjecting the patient to such a traumatic experience if little or no benefit is derived. On the other hand, it is very difficult simply to watch your patient die. So if you feel you must try it as a last resort, use the tube-feeding method recommended in Chapter 1, varying the length and diameter of the tube depending on the species and using a fish and/or meat purée. Take the utmost care with the beak of a long-beaked species. Do not attempt to open or hold the beak open by the tip, but insert the thumbnail between the mandibles near the hinge and prize them gently apart. Hold the beak open by inserting something (a pencil, for example) across the mandibles of the smaller species. The mandibles of a heron can be held open since there is much less danger of damage. Administer the food slowly, and as soon as the operation has been completed, retire from the scene quickly.

If the bird retains the food, then a repetition of the operation is justified, but if it is vomited, the kindest thing is to destroy the bird rather than cause it any further distress.

Symptoms, Diagnosis and Treatment

Injuries. The most common bird in this group to be found injured and requiring help is the heron. The most common injury is to the wing in spite of the fact that the legs look long, fragile and easily injured. Treatment of broken wings is the same as for the waterbirds in Chapter 1.

A useful splint to apply to the very occasional broken leg is a piece of garden hose cut to the correct length and split down the side so that it may be folded over the shaft that is broken. It's useful to pad the limb with a little gauze before you tape the hose in place. Healing occurs in about three weeks or so.

Some herons do not "winter" very well. In a severe winter many may be found dead or suffering from general debility. The best treatment for those still alive is to bring them into warm and dry surroundings and coax them to feed. Often they will perk up fairly rapidly, but while the bad weather lasts, they should be kept indoors and nursed back into full health and vigor.

Injury to shore waders is seldom seen simply because they do not come inland and, when injured, often will fly out to sea to rest. They sometimes suffer from eating contaminated mollusks and may be found debilitated or dead. Treatment consists of giving them activated charcoal to try and absorb the poisonous substances. However, the percentage of success is very small indeed.

Oil Pollution

We have not encountered any of this group suffering from actual oil pollution itself, although, as just mentioned, shore waders can be affected by eating mollusks which have ingested the solvents used to disperse an oil slick.

General Care

Provided it is feeding and has a hiding place to which it can retire at will, keeping a member of this group indoors for a few weeks (three should be ample for most injuries to heal) does no apparent harm. It is always best, though, to get any wild creature out of doors—which is, after all, its natural element—as soon as possible.

*Great
blue heron*

As mentioned in the food section, you may find that a patient from this group will feed only when out of doors, in the quietest possible spot with no people peering at it and with plenty of cover.

A grass paddock or aviary, with plenty of clumps of long grass, shrubs or even weeds and nettles (see Chapter 5), is obviously best. A shallow sunken pool will lend a touch of familiarity for some of the genuine waders. We have had many a convalescent heron stand for hours staring into such a pool although there isn't a fish in sight!

Release

We always feel happiest if a bird will take off from where it has spent its convalescence. This gives a good indication that it feels itself ready to face the world, but such a course isn't always practicable or desirable. It is a good idea to try to return a bird of this group to where it was found or at least to that vicinity. A measure of common sense must be employed, though, because the bird might have been found in an environment completely foreign to its species. If the finding location isn't known or appears completely unsuitable, consult a good bird book on the type of habitat frequented by the particular species you have been treating, and seek out such a spot.

When the convalescent pen *does* make a suitable take-off location and this is the course you decide to adopt, do not be too surprised if your ex-patient hangs around for a long time, showing a marked reluctance to fend for itself. We had one particular heron which spent its convalescence in our waterfowl paddock, where it completely ignored the other residents and spent all its time staring into the pond, as described earlier, showing no inclination to set off into the great wide world, although its broken wing was now perfectly sound. This went on for about a month, with the only activity of the day being a rapid retreat into hiding when one of us approached with a bowl of sprats, followed by an equally rapid reappearance to stuff its beak as soon as we left.

We caught the bird quite often during that month to reexamine the wing. Perhaps it hadn't mended as well as we'd thought and wouldn't support the bird. But all was well, and we heaved a collective sigh of relief when eventually it took off. The following day, however, a visitor asked, "What's that great big bird sitting in a tree over there?" Sure enough, there was our heron, perched incongruously in a tree only a short distance (as the heron flies) from the waterfowl paddock and staring down in that inimitable heron manner. We tried to ignore it, but the accusing stare finally wore us down, and we placed a bowl of sprats in the usual spot, whereupon it promptly flew down, devoured the fish and returned to the tree.

It was a further three weeks before our scrounger finally decided to go and work for itself!

Orphans

Owing to their secretive nature, orphans of this group will seldom be found, the exception being coots and gallinules. We have reared these in the same manner and on the same food as ducklings (see Chapter 1). Indeed, on more than one occasion, an odd gallinule chick has been reared *with* a brood of mallard ducklings. A place to hide must be provided, however, for although the chick will putter about quite happily with the ducklings when no one is around, it will still instinctively run and hide at your approach.

Most of the members of this group are what is called precocial or nidifugous, meaning a bird that leaves the nest immediately or soon after hatching and follows the parent. This being the case, there is no greater chance of survival than if an orphaned infant is allowed to join a group of other precocial infants, albeit of a different species. Indeed, many infants of the group are of a very similar appearance and difficult to tell apart without the presence of an adult bird.

Food like that for ducklings should prove acceptable to all, with the possible addition of fine-minced beef.

The young of the larger members of the group, such as the heron, would require hand feeding. We have never actually encountered such a nestling but would suggest as a suitable diet smallish eels together with the odd dead chick or small rodent, which may have to be chopped up. Although we have fed a good many adult herons on sprats with no apparent ill effects, we would have some reservations in recommending them for rearing a youngster, the sprat being essentially a salt-water fish. There may be no significance in this, but fresh-water fish might be more advisable, even if more difficult to obtain.

There is little risk of imprinting with any of this group, particularly if they are reared with other youngsters. Release can be carried out as for adults when the youngster is fully fledged.

4

Game Birds

Wild turkey

Most people will recognize the pheasant, at least in full plumage, with its long, elegant tail, while the other members of the group are markedly similar to domestic poultry of varying sizes.

Largest, by a fair margin, comes the turkey at anything up to four feet in length and very distinctive in appearance. Did you know that Benjamin Franklin once recommended the turkey to be America's national bird? Much more respectable, he argued, than the bald eagle, which was nothing better than a scavenger!

At the minor end of the scale some of the quail species measure as little as nine inches. Odd man out, in more ways than one, is the roadrunner, that humorous character immortalized in the cartoons. (It doesn't really make a noise like a car horn, by the way.)

Possible Handling Hazards

With everybody and his granddad blazing away at them with guns whenever they poke a tentative beak out of cover, most of the group are very nervous indeed (and who can blame them?), so approaching one that is still mobile can be very difficult. It is best, as always, for several people to help capture the bird as quickly as possible. Some kind of netting—nylon or string fruit netting or fishing net, even a tennis net for the larger species—is invaluable. When the net is pegged out on posts or draped on a hedge, the bird won't recognize it as a barrier and will run straight into it if herded in the right direction. Birds with leg injuries are a fairly simple proposition since they find it almost impossible to get into the air with damaged legs and cannot take advantage of their rapid ground speed.

When captured, birds in this group normally do not attempt to bite, although they will sometimes offer a

rather ineffectual peck or two. A pheasant will sometimes attempt to scratch with its feet in the manner of
a cockerel, but is isn't very good at it. Indeed, most of
this group's efforts are concentrated on trying to escape
rather than putting up a defense. It is necessary to hold
the wings firmly against the bird's body because they
are quite powerful and move so rapidly that the bird
may do itself damage in its frantic efforts to escape.
Unlike other groups which will more or less submit and
stay quiet once they are under restraint, birds in this
group will renew their efforts to escape at the slightest
loosening of the hold and will continue to make the
effort throughout their period of captivity, no matter
how severe the injury.

*Ring-necked
pheasant*

Transportation

Some will sit quietly in a darkened box for a time, but
more often they will thrash about, trying to get out. A
box that offers close confinement is therefore preferable
to one with plenty of room. A soft bag such as a zip-
top shopping or sports bag is quite good, particularly
for a pheasant in full plumage. In any other type of
container the long tail can present something of a problem, but in this type of bag the zipper can be left open
at the end and the tail left protruding. It is best to wrap
the bird (apart from its head) in a piece of cloth or a
towel before placing it in the bag; otherwise it will not
be content with a position of reasonable comfort but
will try to turn around the other way, getting itself tied
up in awful contortions in the process.

Initial Care

The truly wild members of this group will *not* passively
accept a captive state. They will expend great amounts
of energy they perhaps can ill afford, probing for an
escape route. Indeed, their efforts in this respect would
warm the heart of any prisoner of war escapee. If mobile,
they will spend hours simply pacing up and down,
peering at the wall in the hope that an opening may
suddenly appear, and there is really no way to alleviate
this restlessness. It will be more pronounced, though,
when there is a human in sight, so leave the bird alone
as much as possible and try to avoid sudden appearances
which will startle your patient into blind panic, crashing
around and doing itself further injury.

Gray partridge

There is no ideal accommodation for a truly wild member of this group. A warm room offering the least possible sight of people is the best which can be offered in the early stages. Cover the floor with newspaper, and offer food and water.

Food

This, fortunately, should present no problem. The group will eat virtually anything fed to domestic poultry — chick pellets, mixed corn, chopped greens, chickweed, grass, breadcrumbs — and will usually accept food quite readily between escape attempts!

Game birds generally prefer to eat off the ground. If you serve the food in a dish, they are likely to stand in the dish and scratch everything out onto the floor, so you might as well just dump it on the floor in the first place. A bowl of water for drinking should also be provided.

In the unlikely event of your patient's failing to eat, offer some chopped hard-boiled egg to tempt the appetite. A bit of canned dog food will also generally prove acceptable, as will any of the proprietary insectivorous foods.

Roadrunner

Unlike the others, the roadrunner is strictly insectivorous and carnivorous. Dead day-old chicks and mice should prove readily acceptable and are likely to be swallowed whole. Chopped meat, together with mealworms and any other grubs which can be found, will serve for a limited period.

Force-feeding

Force-feeding is not recommended for a member of this group. It should never be necessary, and if your patient should fail to eat at all, there is something radically wrong — damage to the beak, for instance.

Symptoms, Diagnosis and Treatment

Injuries. Predictably the principal injuries suffered by this group are gunshot wounds, which are almost invariably fatal. Occasionally you may see a bedraggled pheasant with disheveled feathers and a drooping wing. It is very difficult to catch such a bird because it tends to run through undergrowth which is often impassable to human beings. But should an injured bird be caught, the first thing to decide is whether the injuries are so extensive that it should be humanely killed. If this is not the case, then the wing should be treated and splinted in a way described in Chapter 1. Broken legs may also be splinted if the break is below the fleshy part of the leg. If it is in the fleshy part, splinting may well allow the leg to heal, but often the joint becomes fixed and the bird is unable to use it. Wounds should be dressed in the way described previously (see pages 9–10), and they tend to heal rapidly.

Some of the group occasionally will run or fly low across a road and be hit by a car. If the bird is alive, it will probably be suffering from shock. The muscles will be twitching, and its eyes will be closed or partly closed. If its neck is not broken and the injuries are not too extensive, a quiet hour or so in a box will generally be sufficient to allow it to recover. If after twelve hours it has not recovered consciousness, it would be better to put it to sleep humanely.

Ruffed grouse

Diseases. Pheasants are susceptible to salmonellosis, psittacosis and mycobacterial diseases, and on postmortem examination they are often found to have been suffering from one or other of these diseases. However, this does not mean to say the pheasant is more susceptible than other wild species. It may well be a result of a captive breeding, for these diseases are also common in pigeons and ducks.

Salmonella is a septicemic type of disease (basically, blood poisoning), and clinical symptoms and indeed the lesions or injuries are not usually sufficiently characteristic to establish a diagnosis. Usually the animal is found dead, but a bird that is showing signs of debility may well be suffering from a chronic type of salmonella.

Psittacosis is a virus disease affecting the lungs and air sacs of many wild birds and, of course, the parrot family, with which it was first associated. It occurs in two forms: the acute, in which the bird is rarely seen alive, and the chronic, which affects a large number of wild birds of many species and has no recognizable symptoms. However, under conditions of stress, birds may develop the acute infection, and they rapidly become weak and dull, lose their appetite, lose weight rapidly and develop diarrhea and a nasal discharge. In most cases death occurs rapidly, probably before a diagnosis has been made. Little can be done in the way of treatment for this disease, and it is better to put the bird to sleep humanely.

Mycobacterial infection or avian tuberculosis also affects pheasants, pigeons, starlings and sparrows—in other words, all the birds that are associated with humans. Primary lesions of tuberculosis are usually in the intestinal tract and may lead to diarrhea. In any case the birds become debilitated with loss of weight and lethargy. There is no treatment for this disease, and when it is diagnosed, the bird should be humanely destroyed. Pheasants are also affected by gapeworm— a worm that lives in the windpipe, causing the bird to develop breathing difficulties and gaping (breathing with the mouth open). This is treatable with the newer worm remedies, such as tetramizole or thiabendazole.

Red grouse are often affected by tiny white threadlike worms in their caeca (parts of their intestines). Some scientists believe that this infection coupled with shortage of food causes many deaths and certainly loss of condition. Yet others say that some grouse in good condition have as many worms and don't seem to be troubled. It is probable that the worms cause disease and death only when the population of grouse is high— there would be greater contamination of the ground and food may be in short supply. The worm, called *Trichostrongylus tenuis*, is susceptible to some of the newer worm treatments, such as Mebenvet, which can be given by mouth.

California quail

General Care

The problems of housing a member of this group, particularly the larger members, do not mellow with time. In fact, the problems during convalescence are even more difficult. When fit, these birds are apt to take off vertically, thereby thumping their heads on whatever is overhead, and they will keep on doing this over and over again until you yourself get a headache just watching them. They will continue to do it when you *aren't* watching them, so it is obviously essential that whatever is overhead be as high as possible, with an absolute minimum of seven feet, preferably eight.

Placed in an aviary, the bird will continue its pacing up and down routine, but this should do no harm since this group does not usually cause damage to itself by probing its beak *through* the wire as some others do.

As mentioned in initial care, there is no *ideal* accommodation for a member of this group. Even tame and domesticated specimens kept in an aviary are apt to try the vertical takeoff if startled, and they will do the same indoors. The only thing to do is offer accommodation with as much headroom as possible and release the bird as soon as you can.

Release

This should preferably be during the closed season for the particular species because you won't be very pleased to have your patient shot immediately on release—and the bird won't be too enthusiastic about it either!

It is preferable to take the bird to an area best suited for its species, where it will fend for itself quite easily on release. Most bird books will give an indication of suitable habitat and areas of distribution. If you don't have or cannot refer to such a book, the area where the bird was found is likely to be satisfactory.

Orphans

It is by no means unusual for a chick of this group to become detached from the rest of the family. It may then be found wandering aimlessly and will almost certainly fall victim to a predator if not rescued. If what appears to be a whole family is found, do not be in too much of a hurry to gather them up because the mother may be in the vicinity. Sometimes the mother's travels take her over a country lane and she may come out of a gate on one side, with the youngsters following, to be confronted by a hedge with no gate on the opposite side. If there isn't a large enough space in the hedge for her to squeeze through, she may fly over and wait on the field side while the youngsters struggle through small gaps in the hedge to join her. Should a car come along during this crossing, the motorist may be confronted by a group of milling chicks, apparently with no parent.

The chicks of this group feed themselves from birth and are therefore easy to feed, although an odd one on its own may prove a problem in that it may continue to look for its lost family, rather than eat. For this reason, it is preferable for the odd youngster to be reared with other chicks, though not necessarily of the same species, and a broody hen will make an excellent foster mother. If no foster mother is available, provide exactly the same accommodation and conditions as for waterfowl youngsters (see Chapter 1).

Chopped hard-boiled egg, chopped grass and/or chickweed, chick starter pellets and an insectivorous food obtainable from any pet shop will make an excellent diet. Budgerigar seed is also acceptable. For roadrunner infants, see notes in the "Food" section.

Do not be in too much of a hurry to put the youngsters outside. Wait until they have a good covering of feathers rather than the down of infancy; otherwise a cold snap or a heavy shower may carry them off. A portable chicken run (see fig. 9) is satisfactory when the chicks move outside, but they should not be considered ready for release until fully fledged, when they can be taken to a suitable site (see "Release").

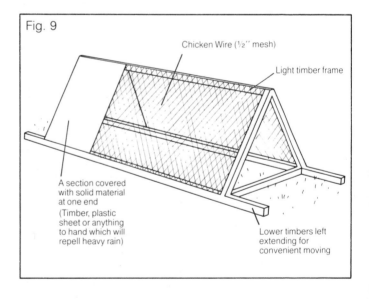

Fig. 9

Chicken Wire (½" mesh)

Light timber frame

A section covered with solid material at one end (Timber, plastic sheet or anything to hand which will repell heavy rain)

Lower timbers left extending for convenient moving

5

Birds of Prey (or Raptors)

Most people will recognize a member of this group, although they may not know which particular species they are looking at. With some thirty-three species of hawklike bird and seventeen owls to choose from, this is hardly surprising, particularly when experienced ornithologists find difficulty in telling some of them apart.

Foot of raptor

The distinctive features common to all of the group are the hooked beak, strong talons and binocular vision (eyes which look to the front and focus together). Largest of the group is the California condor, an immense bird over four feet in length with a nine-foot wingspan (which you are unlikely to encounter and will be fortunate even to see since it is on the verge of extinction). Smallest group member is the American kestrel at a mere one foot. Owls range from the rare (in the United States) great gray at thirty-three inches to the elf (found only in the Southwest) at about six inches.

A great deal of interest and enthusiasm is generated by this group, probably much more than all the others put together, and the reasons are not easy to define. Falconry, of course, accounts for much of the interest, and there can be no denying the thrill of having such a bird return to land on your hand after flying high, wide and free. But there are many, many more people fascinated by a raptor than those engaged in falconry, and fascinated is *not* too strong a term. Could it be the binocular vision, which gives them eyes not unlike our own?

California condor

Owls, particularly, seem to intrigue most people, possibly because of childhood stories of the "wise old owl," but some people aren't too enthusiastic about meeting them face-to-face at close quarters. Among the many we have dealt with over the years were two that spent some time with us, perching all day on a tree branch we had fixed for them in a corner of the office up near the high ceiling (we were very short of aviary space at the time). Most of the day they would sleep, but occasionally they would open their eyes when someone came in and give a few clicks of their beaks, advising the intruders to keep their distance.

On one occasion a dear old lady came in to transact some business or other, and she happened to glance up and see this tree branch with the pair of owls perched thereupon.

"Oh, what a beautiful display," she said admiringly.

Four round eyes suddenly opened wide to stare at her, and two beaks clicked a warning in unison.

"Good heavens, they're alive!" cried the dear old lady as she fled.

Possible Handling Hazards

It is most unusual for a bird in this group to bite, although many will hold their beaks open in a threatening fashion, as though intending to do so, all the time they are being handled. It is the feet which pose the danger. They will defend themselves with their claws, or talons, and will hang on with a viselike grip, often necessitating a second person's being called upon to release the grip.

Depending on the size of the bird involved, damage from the talons can range from a row of small punctures in the skin to a wound requiring several stitches. A grip from the smallest can be painful even if it doesn't do any real damage. There is also a marginally greater danger of a bite from one of the smaller species, but this is likelier with a tame or semitame bird than with a true wild one. Owls will occasionally but not often bite. The greatest danger from an owl is in defense of a nest of young when it can be quite formidable and inflict severe injuries, usually with the talons, on anyone it considers a threat.

Approach and Capture

When first approached, an injured raptor will usually try to hide even if the chosen place of concealment isn't really adequate. The "head in the sand" principle seems to apply. None of the group is very fast on its feet, so in the face of a rapid approach and no (even inadequate) concealment, many will simply crouch down and "play dead." Some will retain this rigid posture—with beak agape—even when picked up, but this cannot be relied on, so the best course is to cover the bird's head with a handkerchief.

A head covering (also covering the eyes, of course) is the only restraint necessary for all of this group, but it is not always easy to achieve. When confronted, the bird is apt to turn over onto its back to fend off the assault with its talons, and trying to drop a handkerchief over the head under these circumstances is rather futile since the bird will keep kicking it away. The safest method is to have the container to be used handy, then to offer the bird a stout stick to grasp. When it has done so, lift it into the container upside down (the container needs to be large enough for the bird to be able to right itself). When the lid is partially closed, cutting off the bird's view of the handler, it will usually release its grip on the stick, allowing it to be withdrawn and the lid fully closed.

Should the bird refuse to grasp the stick—as it may well do—the simplest plan is to cover it completely with a coat or something similar and slowly to ease this back until the talons are revealed and a firm grasp can be taken of the legs. The bird will lie quiet so long as its head is covered, and once the talons have been neutralized, the coat can be withdrawn, another hand placed under the bird, and it can be lifted (slowly and gently) into the container. Try to prevent the bird from grasping one talon with the other during the process because it can do itself virtually as much damage as it can do to you, and this can cause additional problems later.

Transportation

A ventilated cardboard box is all that is needed, even for a large raptor, since the passenger will show no interest in attacking the container. In the absence of a suitable container, the handkerchief simply draped over the head or with two of the points tied together under the beak will be sufficient to keep the bird immobile for as long as necessary. This is precisely the purpose of the ornamental hood worn by birds used in falconry. It should be noted, however, that hooding is inappropriate and indeed unnecessary for owls. An injured owl, placed quite loose in a vehicle, will simply scuttle into a corner or under a seat and is unlikely to cause any problem on the journey.

Short-eared owl

A cautionary note: Wicker cat baskets are not recommended for the transportation of large raptors or any large bird. They usually have very sharp protrusions which do not seem to bother a cat but can cause severe lacerations to a bird.

Initial Care

If the bird has traveled in a box of some sort, you could not do better than to leave it in there overnight in a warm room, unless there should be some urgent reason to do otherwise. It will benefit from the lack of further disturbance at this time, and a move to a more comfortable accommodation can easily be postponed until the following day. Obviously the box must allow for a reasonable amount of movement, including the bird's standing up.

Suitable quarters for a bird of prey are not easy to provide since they can cause themselves damage if the accommodation is wrong. For the time being, until the patient has recovered from whatever brought it to you in the first place, quite restricted quarters, such as a large wooden box which will allow the bird to stand upright on a perch and stretch its wings, will suffice. The perch should be of sufficient thickness to preclude the points of the talons touching the ball of the foot where they can cause injury and lead to further problems. The ends of the box should be covered with paper or cloth to be changed regularly, and the same holds for the base. The reason for the end coverings is that for most of this group, the term *droppings* is not quite appropriate since they are in the habit of leaning forward and shooting out a jet of feces to the rear! The top of the box, from which all servicing can be done, should be covered only with a piece of small mesh nylon netting.

This may seem a sterile, featureless place to keep a bird, and of course, it is, but the less stimulation to movement, the better while an injury is healing, and this group is prone to stand for long periods without movement, even when quite free to move.

Food

A great deal has been written about the care of raptors in captivity, including many ideas on what they should have to eat. Our unequivocal view is that the best possible food you can offer to a member of this group is dead day-old chicks with no additives—no bone meal, no vitamin supplements, no extras at all. We have had dealings with most of the group at one time or another and have dealings with some of them regularly, and in quite large numbers, and all have been fed on this diet with no problems whatsoever, some, we might add, for periods of years.

Unfortunately, because dead day-old chicks are such good food, the casual raptor keeper is likely to experience great difficulty in getting hold of any since they are snapped up from hatcheries by falconers, bird gardens, zoos, etc. In that case you will have to fall back on raw meat with artificially added roughage (fur or feathers). If you can't find anything else, give your dog or cat a brush and use the hairs! A raw meat diet alone is *not* good, but it will do no harm to an adult bird for a short period.

At one time reasonably cheap raw meat could be obtained from pet stores, but this seems harder to get lately. You may therefore have to buy a piece of beef unless you are prepared to scour the roads for bird accident victims, which will meet ready acceptance from most raptors, but the roundup is a rather unsavory pasttime, calling for much dedication! Any meat offered must be in pieces, not minced, but don't hesitate to offer minced meat if nothing else is available.

There is little point in offering a raptor anything other than raw meat (or fish in the case of an osprey) in one form or another, but there is one small consideration. A raptor can go without food for several days with no ill effects, so you don't have to break your neck to get something on the first day. That having been said, though, do not leave it too long because the bird may already have been without food for a day or two before it was found.

Raptors do not normally drink but do enjoy a bath, so if the quarters and any dressings will permit, provide a shallow dish of sufficient size for your patient to have a splash about.

Force-feeding

Possibly we have been lucky, but we have never been obliged to force-feed an adult raptor. Some have gone without food for two or three days, but they all have taken food voluntarily in the end. In view of this experience, it is difficult to suggest circumstances in which we would recommend the practice or consider it essential or even advisable. But one of the early lessons you should learn is that no matter how much you know about wildlife, you don't know everything and are never likely to.

American kestrel

Should force-feeding be contemplated, as always it is best to have two people—one to hold the bird with wings firmly to sides and the other to feed. The talons should be pressed onto a thick wad of cloth or a cushion to prevent their taking part in the proceedings. In spite of its formidable appearance, it is not really difficult to open the beak, and provided you don't force the mandibles too far apart, there is little danger of causing damage. Blunt forceps are best for holding the pieces of food, and for the inexperienced, blunt the tips still further by wrapping a piece of sticky adhesive around each. Place the piece of meat well back on the tongue to start with (later pieces may not need to be so far back once the bird realizes what is happening), close the beak and gently stroke the throat to ensure it is swallowed. You should be able to observe the swallowing action.

Ensure that the pieces of meat, chick or whatever you are using are quite moist by dipping them in water before offering them. It is very difficult to give a firm guide to quantity, but with day-old chicks as a measure, a kestrel that is feeding itself will thrive on a one and two regimen with one fast day—that is to say, one chick on one day and two the next, alternating for six days, and nothing at all on the seventh. A twenty-inch hawk should have twice this amount (a two and four regimen). Use one chick per day for a screech owl and two per day for a short-eared owl, again with a fast day. Others in the group can be gauged from these examples.

Symptoms, Diagnosis and Treatment

Injuries. Birds of prey, in spite of their relative rarity, are often brought for treatment. Perhaps their greatest hazard is persecution by gamekeepers by shooting and pole trapping (a spring trap on top of an upright). In attempting to protect their game birds, many gamekeepers look upon birds of prey as deadly enemies and will do all they can to destroy them. In spite of the fact that it is illegal, pole trapping is still around, and we have seen cases of both feet being severed by such a trap. The birds, of course, had to be destroyed.

Birds of prey are also protected from shooting, but they are still shot, and injured birds are often brought in for treatment. The injuries inflicted are the same as those in other groups, as indeed are the treatments (see pages 9–10). They respond well to captivity, but any broken wing, however, must be perfect when healed, or as near perfect as possible, if the bird is to survive, for it depends entirely on its excellent flight and sight to catch its prey. If the bird is not 100 percent fit and is unable to fly well, it must either be kept in captivity for the rest of its life or be humanely destroyed. It would be cruel to turn this bird loose in the wild and let it starve to death.

Diseases and Poisoning. Some gamekeepers and farmers get rid of birds of prey they think are taking some of their pheasant chicks by poisoning. It is cruel, unnecessary and illegal. Though death from pesticide poisoning is not instantaneous, it is rare to find poisoned birds alive. It is also possible for birds of prey to be affected by taking small mammals that have been poisoned by pesticides. Some poisons accumulate in the body of the bird of prey until there is enough to kill it.

General Care

As mentioned previously, good accommodation for a raptor is not easy to provide, particularly in the convalescent stages, because all of them, when startled, will tend to fly at the wire in an attempt to escape. Owls do reasonably well in the ordinary average aviary. The smaller diurnal raptors *can* be kept in such an aviary, but even they are apt to damage the primary wing feathers and the tail feathers, as well as the cere (the fleshy part of the beak near the face). Larger birds can do serious damage to themselves in such a place.

If an existing aviary is to be used, vertical bars of dowel or cane should be added inside the wire, about two inches in from it and about the same distance apart. If the top is of wire, this should be covered in the same way. There must be somewhere for the bird to hide, so if there is no natural cover (long grass, weeds, foliage), a wooden box with an open end will suffice. Access to one end of the aviary should be denied to people, and the box placed with the opening facing this end, as for the fox enclosure (see fig. 14 on page 127).

If an aviary is to be purposely built, it should be a long rectangle with two of the long sides and one of the short (or even all four) covered in a *solid* material. Translucent fiberglass or heavy plastic sheeting is ideal, but lapboard timber can be used. The height should be a minimum of seven feet, and the top should be of a heavy-gauge small-mesh nylon netting with a covered section of the same material as the sides at the closed end. As with the open aviary, natural cover or a hiding box should be available so the bird can retire from view when you enter the aviary. Perches should not be too high, allowing plenty of headroom when the bird takes off and lands, and the perches should be of varying thickness but not too thin for the species concerned (see "Initial Care" and "Symptoms, Diagnosis and Treatment").

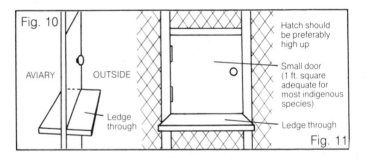

If neither of the above alternatives is possible, a clean clutter-free shed would offer the best alternative with the window barred as above. Although we would not recommend it for permanent accommodation, a raptor can live in a shed for a lengthy period with no apparent ill effects, but be sure to provide regular bathing facilities.

Release

It is strongly urged that a raptor be released directly from the convalescent quarters. In this way, it has an orientation point where it can, and very often will, return for food in the initial difficult period of readjustment to the wild. Some rehabilitated raptors will continue to return sporadically for weeks or even months after release, and they must always be sure of a meal if they do, so a sharp lookout must be kept for their reappearance in the vicinity.

It is patently impossible to maintain a permanent watch for a returning bird, but we found that if we fed a patient at a regular time each day for the entire period of treatment and convalescence, it tended to reappear at about the same time of day after release. If there is any sign of it in the vicinity, food can then be placed on the roof of the aviary or shed or on the ledge of the release hatch, if one has been provided (see figs. 10 and 11).

If the premises where the bird is being treated is not a desirable release point, we would suggest it be transferred elsewhere for its period of convalescence. Please do not simply take the bird somewhere and release it cold, no matter how quiet the spot chosen. Raptors have a hard enough row to hoe when released, and many *need* that backup of a place where they know food will be available.

Cooper's hawk

Orphans

Finding a young bird apparently all alone is not sufficient reason for assuming it to be an orphan and carting it home. In the case of a raptor, such a course might well result in a torn scalp or even a lost eye from the attack of an irate parent. There is, in fact, no easy formula for determining whether or not a particular infant has been abandoned, but in general, we would advise leaving it where it is found and not touching it at all. This may seem rather callous, but there is no doubt at all that the vast majority of *assumed* orphans are nothing of the sort.

Of course, there are many circumstances in which youngsters simply must be rescued. For instance, most of our raptor chicks arrive as a result of tree felling, which is just a bit much even for staunch raptor parents to countenance. In one recent season we had no fewer than twenty-two newly hatched owlets brought in during such operations, and most years produce at least a couple of families of one species or another.

Raptor infants are very easy to rear. As for the adults, we strongly recommend day-old chicks, which must, of course, be chopped up and preferably dampened with water. The size of the pieces obviously depends on the species, but you will find that a young raptor can swallow pieces much larger than you would imagine. During its first few weeks, indeed, it will eat much more than an adult of the same species, so keep on offering pieces until the bird has had enough. It will usually indicate this by holding the last piece in its beak for a time and then dropping it.

Barn owl

Offer food about four or five times a day, and don't worry about set times. Owlets, for instance, will accept food and thrive just as well if fed during the day, so there is no point in losing any sleep by feeding during the night.

If this sounds rather casual, that's because it is! For this group there is no need at all for rigid regimen or more frequent feedings. Raptors, even very young ones, are equipped to go without food for long periods. This is quite logical if you give it some thought. All their food has to be *caught*. In other words, it is all very much alive and "on the hoof," not just waiting around to provide sustenance for madam raptor and family. Even on nice days (or nights) the collection of food is a chancy business (apart from a fair percentage of beetles, which are somewhat easier to catch). Consider the problems on a foul, stormy day, of which we claim in Britain to get more than our fair share, and you will appreciate why raptors and their offspring can manage—and, indeed, do manage—on a somewhat irregular diet.

At first the youngster's beak may have to be opened and the pieces of food popped well in, either with blunt forceps or just with the fingers, but most of them learn very quickly and will take hold of the food themselves when it is dangled before their beaks. If day-old chicks cannot be obtained and you have to use raw meat, add a sprinkling of bone meal to each feed, and don't forget to add some kind of roughage—cat or dog hair or even hair from an old spare wig or toupee, if you happen to use such an adornment!

It is difficult if you're rearing only a single youngster to avoid some measure of imprinting, but there are a few simple rules which should be rigidly adhered to if the bird is to have the optimum chance of surviving when released. The same rules apply, of course, if you raise more than one. Touch the bird or birds as little as possible. Never stroke or caress them in any way (some enjoy this, so it is a great temptation). Never talk to them. It's better (for them) at a later date that the sound of a human voice should frighten rather than encourage them.

As soon as the youngsters can feed themselves, try to prevent them from seeing just where the food comes from. This is to try to stop the association of humans with food, and it may call for some ingenuity, depending on the setup. In the early hand-feeding stage the young can be kept in a box, even a cardboard one, anywhere about the house, and there is no need to provide artificial heat unless the ambient temperature drops very low (for the time of year). Our experience is that they will move away from artificial heat, so if in doubt, provide the heat, but allow the opportunity to move away from it. By the way, do not provide bathing facilities until the youngsters change their down for feathers.

The remarks regarding prerelease and release of adult casualties apply also to hand-reared infants. In fact, we consider quarters from which they can be released directly to be absolutely essential if the birds are to stand the optimum chance of survival. Feeding, too, should now be at a regular time (see "Release").

There is a view quite commonly held that hand-reared raptors must be "trained" to catch their food. We do not subscribe to this view. The so-called training that some rearers believe in consists of introducing live mice to the aviary or prerelease quarters for the bird to kill and eat. We hold that this is not training at all but merely offers the bird an opportunity to exercise the predatory instincts it *already possesses*. Of course, it must acquire skills in hunting, but this sterile practice is no substitute for the real thing. The bird must acquire the necessary knowledge for survival *in the field* but with the backup of an orientation point where food is available to supplement early inefficiency.

"That's all very well," say the doubters, "but how do you know your methods work? How do you know that when the birds stop coming back for food, they haven't just died?" Good and reasonable questions to which we would reply by quoting just one case (of many). The twenty-two owlets mentioned earlier all were released from the same point at the same time, and all were wearing officially marked bands, which made them easily indentifiable. None was ever picked up, dead, dying or otherwise. Surely even the most skeptical must concede that if such a bunch had come to grief, at least one would have been recovered. By the way, one of this lot was still returning for an occasional meal two months after release!

Just when to effect the release is a rather difficult problem. Most people who have successfully reared any wild creature are reluctant when it comes to the final step, and this is quite understandable. It's a very harsh world out there. In the case of your young raptor or raptors, allow about four weeks *after* the birds are fully fledged, and make the release preferably during a settled spell of fine weather or at least on a fine day. Diurnal species should be released in the early morning, nocturnal in the late evening (but while it is still light). If you have a release hatch, this is simply left open at feeding time. As with adult releases, have a good look around at this time each day after release, and don't stop doing so just because the bird has failed to appear for several days. Give it at least a fortnight from the last appearance before assuming it isn't coming back.

Speaking of raptors reminds us of a certain lady visitor to our wildlife hospital. She asked if we had a parrot she could buy and was told that we didn't sell birds, and in any case we kept only indigenous birds.

"Oh," she said, wrinkling her nose, "I wouldn't want one of those horrible things that only eat meat."

With great self-restraint, we reserved our hilarity until she left the premises!

We must admit, though, the laugh is quite often at our own expense, like a recent occasion at Bill's house. Bill was sitting quietly reading late at night after the rest of the family had retired when his son crept in, alarmed and apprehensive.

"There's somebody in the attic," he whispered. "I can hear him snoring."

Bill went to investigate and, sure enough, could hear a rattly intake of breath and a gasping exhalation. It certainly sounded like somebody up there, and the worse for drink, too, by the sound of him, but how on earth had he managed to get up there without anyone's seeing him?

Intrepid Bill climbed up to take a look, but there

was nobody there, yet they could still hear the snoring. Bill began to think along the lines of the supernatural, as one is apt to do with inexplicable noises at dead of night, when he suddenly remembered that a barn owl had been occupying a dove cote which was fixed just above the attic. It was making the row! But Bill had to make a thorough search of the attic before his son would believe him.

6

Other Birds

This chapter may be considered too wide-ranging in that it deals with a very large number of species, but there are several reasons why we have lumped them all together. The first is that in spite of the wide variety of species included, they do have one thing in common — namely, they all are altricial or nidicolous (that is to say, birds that stay in the nest after hatching and are fed by the parents until fledged). The birds of prey of the previous chapter are, of course, also altricial, as are some of those in Chapters 2 and 3 and some which have traits of both altricial and precocial species, but raptors are a somewhat specialist group, while those appearing in the other chapters fall more readily into the groups we have selected for them than into this chapter.

Mockingbird

A second reason is that although there are so many, and any of them *could* at some time appear as casualty or orphan, in practice very few do. Probably the main reason is that most of the species very sensibly conduct their affairs at a discreet distance from the human race. The principal casualties and orphans we have received from this group over the years are those commonly called garden birds or others that do not fall strictly into this category but nonetheless live in close proximity to humans. This is not to say that accidents and injuries do not happen to those living farther afield, because they certainly do, but the incidence is undoubtedly much less where people are not involved, as are the chances of being rescued. One of these casualties is much more likely to make the next meal for some other creature on the lookout for just such a treat.

In silhouette, most of the group look very much alike, with all principal features modestly proportioned in relation to the bird's size. There are "odd men out," such as the swifts, kingfishers, hummingbirds and one or two more, whose outlines look somewhat different. Size ranges from the common raven at about twenty-seven inches to the calliope hummingbird at three inches or less, and the grouping covers some 300 species.

Possible Handling Hazards

Most of this group will attempt to bite when handled, and the strength of the bite does not necessarily relate to the bird's size. Some of the finches, for instance, can give quite a painful nip, sufficient to cause the unwary handler to drop the bird, whereas, say, the thrushes, at about twice the size, have a very mild, harmless bite. This is due in the main to the feeding preferences of the particular birds. A bird that feeds principally on seeds has a much stronger beak than one that eats mainly insects, and this leads to the general classification of the two groups as hardbills and softbills. The difference between the two can be appreciated when one has hold of your finger!

Common crow

The raven has a formidable bite and is best handled with gloves. The other larger members of the crow family also have quite strong bites but not usually sufficient to break the skin, while the smaller members do not have much of a bite but are apt to rap off a series of pecks with the sharp tip.

Although, apart from the raven, there is little or no danger of serious injury from a bird in this group, it is worth repeating the warning: *No bird should ever be held near the handler's face.*

Approach and Capture

The most general reaction from this group when approached is to escape, although some will try to hide at first and only break and flee at the last moment, when you are almost upon them. Since the vast majority of the group are under ten inches, with a high proportion only half this length, they can be quite difficult to catch without exacerbating the injury and adding to the shock they will already be suffering.

A catching net (see fig. 1, page 4) is a positive boon for this job, but if none is available, it is best to try to drop something over the bird. A coat is suitable for the larger species, such as crows or pigeons, but for the small birds, it should be something lightweight, such as a towel or even a T-shirt. Alternatively try trapping the bird under a cardboard box to which a pole or branch can be easily attached (fig. 12), allowing the catching to be done without coming right up to the bird and causing it to flee.

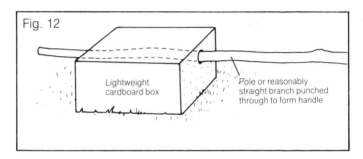

Fig. 12

Lightweight cardboard box

Pole or reasonably straight branch punched through to form handle

Whatever you use to trap the bird, it should be removed very slowly until the bird can be grasped with its wings at its sides, then lowered slowly into the traveling container. Avoid rapid or jerky movements, which will only cause panic, and try to support the feet during the move (when a bird doesn't feel its feet touching anything, it assumes it must be flying and will instinctively try to flap its wings).

Some of the crow family may have a go at the container, and the larger of them can certainly penetrate the average cardboard box with a little diligent work. But unless the journey is very long, and the bird is suffering only a minor injury which doesn't hinder its excavations, it is unlikely to make a large enough hole through which to escape before you reach your destination.

At the other end of the scale, some of the smaller birds can be carried in a paper bag (with air holes, of course), with little danger of their escaping or even trying to escape. The general rule for this group is that they can be carried in anything large enough to contain them.

Initial Care

Rest, peace and quiet, and warmth are the first essentials. For the smaller species there are specially designed hospital cages which are quite good, but any kind of

cage or box which can be covered to keep it dark will
suffice for the first twenty-four hours. Even a covered
hot-water bottle near your patient is better than nothing. A temperature of around 77° F (25° C) should be
aimed for, or even up to 86° F (30° C) if there is any
way of grading the temperature and the bird is sufficiently mobile to choose its own spot.

*American
robin*

It is also desirable that the bird be given some fluid
in these early stages. Warm water by itself is a great
deal better than nothing, but if a pinch of glucose can
be added, this will be most beneficial. You can use an
eyedropper for this purpose, but by far the best thing
to use is a plastic syringe (without the needle, of course).
The actual quantity is not really critical: a few drops
for a finch and half a teaspoon for a crow, repeated at
about two-hour intervals (but not during the night,
when the bird should be left completely alone). The
fluid is best administered at the hinge of the beak, a
little at a time since care must be taken that none enters
the glottis (which leads to the lungs). If the bird is
allowed to breathe freely between drops, there is little
danger of this happening. If the bird is panting, oral
administration of fluids should not be attempted. There
are more beneficial ways of administering fluids detailed
under "Symptoms, Diagnosis and Treatment."

On the second day the bird should be moved to quarters with more light, where it can be offered food and
water, but the ambient temperature should still be warm.
The quarters should offer a secluded spot and enough
room to move around and stretch the wings. Depending
on the particular patient, this can be anything from a
small cage to a whole room.

Food

Many are the weird and wonderful recipes for the feeding
of wild birds in captivity, and indeed, no stone should
be left unturned in the effort to get your patient to eat.
The turning of stones can be taken literally, by the way,
since a good many of this group will appreciate a nice
fat snail.

As mentioned earlier, most birds in this group are
either insect eaters or seed eaters, or more likely a com-
bination of both, with a preference for one or the other.
Different beak shapes give a clue to this preference, but

virtually all cross the dividing line from time to time when something on the other side takes their fancy or when their preferred food is in short supply.

Mountain bluebird

Insectivorous foods are available at pet stores, and softbills may also accept canned dog or cat food mixed with breadcrumbs, chopped bacon rind, cheese, fine-chopped or minced raw meat, corned beef, plus any worms or snails that might be lurking about and even a few flies (but *not* those you've knocked off with a fly spray). Hardbills in general will accept food in captivity more readily than softbills and can be given breadcrumbs, chopped greens and apple, plus budgerigar seed or indeed any other seed, including grass seed (take care that it hasn't been treated to repel birds). Most species in the group will accept chopped hard-boiled or scrambled eggs, and many will readily accept a little fish such as canned fish (in tomato sauce or water rather than oil).

The larger crows can do with more meat. Canned dog food is acceptable, but a dead day-old chick will be very much appreciated, as will any other meat or bones to pick at. A whole chicken or turkey carcass, after you've had your share, will be a veritable feast.

There are one or two specialists in the group that will require special catering. The woodpeckers and tree creepers should be provided with a nice thick (and preferably rotting) upright log, which they can explore for beetles and grubs. We have also had some success with these by plastering a mixture of insectivorous food and canned dog food onto the log. Kingfishers need small fish, and we usually use whitefish for this species (see "Force-feeding"). Dried flies can *usually* be obtained from pet stores for flycatchers, and these can be supplemented with any house or garden flies, a worm or two and any grubs you can find. Folded leaves on trees and bushes often yield a rich harvest of grubs. For swifts, see "Force-feeding."

Most people are aware that hummingbirds feed on nectar from flowers, but less generally known is the fact that they also consume large quantities of small insects. Artificial nectar made of sugar and water, preferably with added glucose, will sustain a bird for a strictly limited period (no more than a few days). If one needs to be kept for a longer period because of injury, several additions, such as Hydramin and Gevral, need to be made to the diet, and while these can easily be obtained, it would probably be in the bird's best interest if you passed it on to someone better equipped to deal with it. A culture of fruit flies is, for instance, necessary for long-term care. Honey is frequently used in artificial nectar but is suspect (it may cause a fungal disease), and we do not recommend its use.

We have not handled every species in this group; indeed, it is doubtful if *anybody* has. It is easy to find out what any particular species eats in the wild since most bird books give you this information. Getting the same species to eat in captivity, when injured, is quite a different matter. Do not be afraid to experiment, for the bird is unlikely voluntarily to eat anything which will do it harm, and do not allow your patient's food preference in the wild to dominate your thinking. A bird that normally eats flies might easily enjoy a portion of plum pudding! Water should, of course, be provided for all. See also the notes about dishes and methods of presentation in the food section of Chapter 3.

Cardinal

Force-feeding
No animal (including ourselves) enjoys the experience of being forcibly fed, and if you couple this lack of enthusiasm for the actual operation with an abject fear of the creature doing it, you should get indication of the bird's side of the matter. So don't force-feed birds in this group unless you are obliged to as a last resort.

Swifts will not normally feed themselves in captivity, but it is quite easy to force-feed them because they have mouths almost big enough to take a side of beef! Although they may be kept alive and may grow accustomed to a captive state (they appear to have little or no fear of humans), the chances of an injured swift's being able to return to its singular mode of life are very slim indeed (see "Release").

Do not expect uniformity of behavior, even with birds of the same species. Some kingfishers, for instance, will pick fish out of a bowl of water, others will grab and swallow a fish handed to them (head first), others will swallow a fish placed just in the beak (again head first), while still others will need to have the fish pushed down their throats.

Obviously you must be more selective when force-feeding to choose something near the bird's normal food range since it isn't taking the meal voluntarily, thereby making its own selection. A good starter, which will be satisfactory for most in this group, would be fine-grated hard-boiled egg mixed with dampened bread-crumbs or scrambled egg by itself. The former can be made into pellets of a suitable size of the bird in question; the latter, offered just in pieces.

The food may have to be placed well back on the tongue with the aid of blunt forceps or tweezers, and a good trick is to follow each piece with a drop or two of water from a syringe or small paintbrush, which will encourage the bird to swallow (see "Initial Care").

Never try to open a beak by the tip; always open it near the hinge, and always handle the beak very carefully to avoid the risk of distortion.

Symptoms, Diagnosis and Treatment

Injuries. The most frequent injury in this group is mauling by domestic cats, which causes shock and both internal and external injuries. Broken wings, broken legs and concussion caused by collision with cars or windowpanes are also fairly common. These accidents occur most commonly in the late spring and early summer, when the youngsters are leaving the nest and are not very "worldly-wise."

House sparrow

On examination the bird may show no external injuries but appears to be dead and is limp, both wings outspread and eyes closed. But when you pick it up, you can feel its heart beating. Unfortunately many of them, especially those mauled by a cat, will not regain consciousness, for this is a particularly traumatic experience for a little bird. Those that fly into a window-pane or are hit by a car may recover, provided the neck is not broken or extensive internal injuries have been caused. The simplest form of treatment is to place the bird in a little open box lined with tissue and put it in a dark, quiet place until it has recovered. It is best to put the small box containing the unconscious bird inside a larger closed box or cage; otherwise it may well recover and start flying at the windows, trying to get out of the room in which you have kept it. It can also be examined from time to time without upsetting the bird, which can easily be released when it has recovered.

Shock may be simply a loss of consciousness owing to dissociation (a sort of blockage to the relay system) in the brain caused by a blow, such as flying into a window. It is analogous to a knockout in the boxing ring, and normally the bird should recover. If the neck is broken, however, it will certainly die without regaining consciousness.

The shock caused by a cat mauling is different. Dilation of the blood vessels—brought on by the mental anguish of being caught by a predator—causes a slowing of the heart rate and a fall in blood pressure. In nature this shock serves a very useful purpose because many prey animals caught by predators lose consciousness and thus are insensitive to the injuries subsequently inflicted. Death may occur because of the shock itself, or the bird may hemorrhage later.

American goldfinch

The treatment for this form of shock is to increase the volume of the circulating blood by giving drugs that stimulate the heart and contract the blood vessels or by giving fluids that will be absorbed into the blood system, also increasing its volume. The layperson can only give fluids by mouth—provided the bird is able to swallow, and for this it must be conscious—whereas the veterinarian can give (or instruct a layperson) on how to give fluids by injection into the vein, into the peritoneal cavity or even under the skin, which will help increase blood pressure and counteract the shock. These injections are either blood replacers specially prepared for that purpose or a 5 percent solution of glucose sterilized for injection.

Again, put the bird in a dry, not too warm box in the dark, and leave it alone for a quiet hour or so, by which time it should have recovered. It is important not to disturb the bird too often once it has recovered. When it is conscious, if the injuries are slight, the bird can be released. But if it still appears to be weak, then you should attempt to give it a small amount of fluid containing glucose (at about 1 percent concentration— roughly a heaped teaspoon—to 1 pint [600 milliliters] water). A bird should *never* be released to the wild until it is strong and fit enough to fly; otherwise it will be subject to attack by ground predators and may not survive.

Sometimes the brain is damaged, usually by a hemorrhage or blood clot in the nervous tissue. Symptoms are a partial paralysis of one side of the bird or of a wing or limb or a circling movement, in which the bird continually flutters or staggers around with its head bent in the direction of the circling. Prognosis is bad, and it is kinder to put the bird to sleep if it shows no improvement in twenty-four hours. Broken wings and legs are not uncommon, but because many of these birds do not rely on *perfect* flight to obtain their food, being mainly seed and insect eaters, it is possible for them to get about perfectly well with a slightly crooked wing or leg, and some can manage with only one leg.

Do not be too quick to discard an apparently dead hummingbird. The bird conserves energy by a state of torpidity at night, and while it is in this state, it is not unusual for one to be blown off its perch in a high wind. Warming in the hands is frequently all that is necessary in such cases.

Diseases and Poisoning. Poisoning can occur from time to time when the plants upon which these birds feed are contaminated with insecticides. Fruit tree and garden sprays and some agricultural sprays are particularly hazardous, and cases where a number of small birds have been found dead have been reported. Always use any spray very carefully to minimize the ever-present risk. Little can be done with this kind of poisoning even if the birds are found alive. There is no specific antidote, and careful nursing is the only treatment. It is usually too late to administer fluids to wash out the poisons, which are very rapidly absorbed.

Starling

Symptoms of disease in birds are of such a general nature that they seem to apply to a number of diseases. More often than not diagnosis cannot be made on symptoms alone. But many species of these garden birds are susceptible to the common bird diseases. Psittacosis in its chronic form is particularly prevalent in such birds as sparrows and pigeons. Tuberculosis can affect pigeons, sparrows and starlings, and salmonellosis has been found in pigeons and crows. As is the case with most wild creatures, the symptoms are not evident either until the disease is advanced and little can be done or until the animal is shocked or placed under stress by some other catastrophe which precipitates the acute form of the disease and rapid death.

Nearly every wild creature, bird or mammal, carries internal and external parasites, but provided the bird is living a natural life with a reasonable amount of food, no untoward effects can be seen. Should food supplies diminish, water supplies dry up in a drought season or there be a severe winter, disease symptoms may become manifest, and they usually progress rapidly to death.

If a conscious wild bird can be picked up fairly readily, you can be certain that something is seriously wrong with it. If there are no signs of injury, then it is quite likely to be suffering from disease. Diagnosis is difficult for the veterinarian and almost impossible for the layperson. Treatment will be almost useless for the individual bird because it may have been hiding the symptoms of the disease for some time before it became ill.

The best treatment for these cases is to keep the bird warm—approximately 77° F (25° C)—and provide it with a plentiful supply of the correct food and water. If it is suffering from a disease that is far advanced, then it will die fairly quickly. If not, there is a good chance that it will recover, and once able to fly, it may be released.

Two examples that are fairly typical of an ordinary member of the public's being involved with wild bird care, one with a happy ending, the other not, show the vicissitudes of nature. In the middle of a very bad winter a young man found the smallest of British birds, the goldcrest, sitting outside a greenhouse, looking cold and dejected. It was fairly easy to open the greenhouse door and slowly and carefully drive the little fellow inside. A frantic search was then made for some insects for the bird to eat, and a few were found. These were offered on a saucer and readily taken. The bird then began hopping about, in the course of which it hopped onto the young man's shoe and cocked an eye up at him. There were high hopes that it would recover, and everyone searched for more insects and brought a heater in to warm the greenhouse. The goldcrest fed until it was dark, but because it was midwinter, darkness came early and the night was long. The next day it was found dead, causing much sadness and disappointment. And there was no obvious reason why the bird died.

On another occasion a blackbird was taken to a vet for treatment with a badly smashed wing. Both the radius and the ulna had been broken in more than one place, and the wing flopped about loosely. The skin was broken on the inside, and it had been bleeding. But the bird was not shocked, seeming to accept its human

Western meadowlark

companions, and would eat food offered in the hand. The wing was treated and then strapped to the bird's body. Thereafter careful nursing by the woman who found it effected a complete recovery, for when she brought it back and the strapping was removed, it flew about the room almost normally. She kept it a few more days and then finally released it into the garden and was delighted when it used to return each day to her bird table to be fed from her hand. One bird at least had learned that humans need not always be feared.

General Care

The plumage of many of this group is apt to deteriorate or become badly soiled if the bird is kept indoors for very long, so it is strongly recommended that as soon as possible your patient be moved out of doors, where the plumage can "weather" normally. If you cannot provide a suitable aviary, do not be possessive, but pass the bird on to someone who can.

Most of the smaller members of this group will benefit in convalescence from the reassuring presence of other birds about them, albeit of other species. They will fare quite happily in an aviary of budgerigars, foreign finches or even some of the smaller parakeets (although care and sound advice must be taken with the latter since some species of parakeet are rather pugnacious). We keep a number of resident budgerigars in our aviaries specifically to fulfill this therapeutic function.

Crows can be kept with other members of the same family or with any other birds large enough to "hold their own," such as pheasants, although it might be judicious to keep ravens on their own.

The field is wide if you are intending to build your own aviary, but one or two points should always be incorporated. Never place the aviary in such a way that people can walk all around it. This is very traumatic for a bird, even one accustomed to being in an aviary, because such conditions may completely deprive it of its flight line (the distance at which a bird feels safe from a human). Allow sufficient headroom. It is important when you enter the aviary that the bird should be able either to hide or to get above your head (allow seven feet minimum). Allow a bit of cover from heavy rain (heavy plastic sheeting, for example), but do not cover the whole top with solid material. Within the

Black-capped
chickadee

limits of the materials available, increase the length at the expense of the width. In other words, a long rectangle is preferable to a square, provided you allow people to approach only at one end and not walk around the sides, too. This will enhance the flight line, adding to the bird's peace of mind and assisting recuperation. A grass base is preferable for all of this group, although you will have to introduce sand or gravel at favorite sitting spots as the grass becomes soiled with droppings.

Release

With about 300 species in the group, it is difficult to generalize about how and where release should be effected. As with the shearwaters mentioned in Chapter 2, some birds thought to be casualties are merely birds that have inadvertently become grounded and cannot take off from flat ground. The swift is such a bird, with swallows and martins also suffering from the same problem to some extent. Such a grounded bird may need only a boost into the air in order to be on its way.

The trouble with releasing rehabilitated casualties of this group from an urban aviary is that you can never be quite sure what the bird will do when released. It may fly away rapidly on release and may well reach a suitable habitat under its own steam, long before you could reach the same spot by car. On the other hand, a "country" bird released from an aviary in the middle of a city may have some difficulty in orientating itself and may fall easy prey to a cat. On balance, it is probably best to take the bird to an area best suited to its species, and most bird books will furnish you with this knowledge.

The bird books will also tell you whether your bird is a resident or migratory species and, if the latter, whether it should have already left the country. You may have to consider keeping the bird until the following spring, and this can certainly be done.

Orphans

Nestlings can come to hand in a variety of ways, but the most common is someone chopping down a tree or taking the roof off a building at the wrong time. If there is any possibility of the nest's being saved *in situ*, this should be done since the parents will almost certainly continue feeding the family if given a reasonable

Nestlings gaping for food

opportunity to do so. In many cases this simply isn't possible, and hand rearing has to be undertaken. Fortunately the nestlings of this group all gape for their food, and it is a fairly easy, if arduous, task to feed them. Most will open their beaks at the slightest sound of any sort; some will open up only at a slight tap on the edge of the nest or if you make a soft, hissing sound.

In the circumstances described above, it may be possible to rescue the nest as well as the nestlings, in which case they should continue to live in it. If the nest has been destroyed, you must construct one which resembles the original as closely as possible, meaning round in shape, small enough to keep the youngsters close together, and with sides high enough to stop them falling out. A round container ranging from the bottom of a plastic dishwashing liquid bottle to a cookie tin, depending on the species, lined with paper towels, should prove satisfactory. It is not advisable to use an old nest because this may contain some undesirable residents.

The nestlings will require warmth, at least until they get their feathers and thereafter at nights until they leave the nest. A temperature in the region of 86° F (30° C) is necessary, but since these infants cannot move away if too hot, take some trouble over the placing of the heat source and keep a close eye on the reaction of the infants. An infrared lamp placed at a certain height over the nest may be just right during the night but may rapidly get too hot on a very warm day. In too high a temperature the infants will be making obvious efforts to move away from each other with necks stretched out; they may pant as well. When too cold, their bodies will feel cold to the touch.

A bit of thought should also be given to where the nest is placed. The reason is that the youngsters should remain in the same quarters until they are feeding themselves and they will want to be out of the nest and hopping about before then. So if, when they start leaving the nest, they are immediately moved somewhere else — to an aviary perhaps — they may panic in the new surroundings when approached and fail to come for food. If they are kept in the same room as the nest, this is unlikely to happen, and they will continue to gape for the person who has reared them (although they may not for a stranger).

In the wild all these nestlings, including the seed

eaters, are fed largely on insects, and we have found a mixture of insectivorous food and dampened bread-crumbs to be satisfactory for most. Canned dog or cat food is also acceptable. Very young birds of the smaller species are usually started on sieved hard-boiled egg yolk, mixed to a paste with a little water and served with a small artist's paintbrush. Crushed crackers can be added to the egg yolk (the mixture can be obtained commercially) for slightly larger youngsters.

Brown thrasher

When you use the insect/breadcrumb formula, the mixture should be firm enough to make into pellets, which will vary in size according to species. A finch will take pellets about a half inch long by one-eighth inch diameter, while a crow will comfortably manage one inch long by one-half-inch diameter. To save giving water separately as well as to help them go down easily, dip each pellet in water just before offering it to the bird. "Bald" infants should be fed *at least* every half hour from dawn till dusk and be given as much as they will take at each feeding. It is impossible to overfeed nest-lings, for they will stop gaping when they have had enough each time, and this is a big help in sorting out just who has been fed when there are several in the nest. They will also defecate after a feed, and because the dropping is covered with a fine skin, it can be picked up from the nest with a pair of tweezers before it makes a mess of both nest and birds—although we do not advocate swallowing it, as the parent birds frequently do!

The nestlings will grow very rapidly and will soon be clambering up the sides of the nest. The length of time they will need to be hand-fed is very difficult to define exactly (even within a species), for most are still fed by their parents for some time after leaving the nest. As soon as the youngsters begin to get around, leave some of the same food in the vicinity for them to peck at, as they will do very inefficiently at first, and grad-ually cut down the number of feedings to four a day. This should be maintained until they are fully self-sufficient, at which time most will cease to beg for food at your approach. The crow family is particularly dif-ficult to break off. Crows should continue to be hand-fed for at least two weeks after leaving the nest, and whatever they manage to pick up themselves will need to be supplemented for about another two, after which hand feedings should be few and far between to encourage them to fend for themselves.

All too frequently people pick up fledglings that have fallen a few days prematurely from the nest or that have recently vacated it. These are a vastly different proposition from nestlings and, as a general rule, should be left where they are found. The parents will almost certainly continue to feed the youngster and will do a much better job of it than the finder is likely to do. The problem is that it is difficult to make such a decision in any given circumstances, and it is quite impossible to generalize. Take the case of an almost-fledged bird that has managed to fall out of a nest in an urban area. Even if the parents do continue to feed it, the chances are that it will fall prey to one of the many cats that undoubtedly prowl the neighborhood. Since you know the location of the nest, it might seem like a good idea to climb up and put the youngster back, but to do so would almost certainly cause the others to explode from the nest in panic, thereby making the problem much worse.

Scissor-tailed flycatcher

The best course in such circumstances is to place the youngster in a box which it cannot easily jump out of but which affords access for the parents and to set the box in a sheltered position off the ground near the nest but without disturbing it. The parents will almost certainly find the youngster and continue to feed it. You can in any case keep watch from a distance to ensure that they do, and the youngster can follow the parents out when it is fully fledged. Ordinary birdcages have frequently been used for this purpose, and the parents have continued to feed the caged youngster through the bars, even when the cage is taken indoors at night and put out only through the day. In this case the youngster has to be released manually, when judged ready.

There are undoubtedly many cases in which the only recourse is to attempt the rearing of a fledgling, but it is much more difficult than raising it from the nestling stage and should not be lightly undertaken. The problem is that a bird's innate fear of humans is already manifest by the fledgling stage, but it is not yet ready to feed itself. Each feeding is, therefore, a struggle between hunger and terror, with the bird having to be caught and held and force-fed each time. Not the best of starts, and one that often ends in disaster with the bird dying. If you are obliged for any reason to try it, the notes on force-feeding adults apply (see page 63).

It is difficult to give any hard-and-fast rules regarding the release of hand-reared youngsters of this group. You must not release them prematurely, but you must release them in plenty of time to prepare for migration if they are of a migratory species, and you must release them in time to ensure a reasonable period of complete self-sufficiency before winter sets in if they are a resident species. The optimum time is early to midsummer, when nature intended it. Occasionally a bird of this group will stay in the vicinity after release, in which case you can continue to provide food, but most will leave immediately.

7

Oil Pollution

In the field of cleaning and rehabilitating birds contaminated with oil, there are quite a number of people who "know how to do it," and indeed, some perform a very good job. Unfortunately many don't, and they bring into disrepute the whole endeavor, an endeavor which already suffers from a distinct lack of credibility in many quarters. A number of critics flatly refuse to believe that a bird can be returned to 100 percent buoyancy after being cleaned. Others say that even if it can be done, the birds do not survive after being returned to the sea, and even more claim the whole exercise is of no significance anyway because of the very small numbers which can be saved from any incident. We have been engaged in this work for a number of years, using methods devised originally by the Zoology Department of Newcastle University, and can claim to have achieved some success in answering the doubters.

In the case of birds contaminated with most crude oils we can, without any reservation, achieve a return to 100 percent buoyancy (that is, where no water can penetrate the feathers) in a period measured only in days. This we have demonstrated to many who doubted it could be done. Long-term survival is much more difficult to prove, relying as it does on birds being picked up again after their return to sea, which, of course, can happen only when the bird is once more in difficulties of some sort. A bird that has returned to a normal life is unlikely to be picked up again; this applies particularly to seagoing birds like auks.

Of the many birds we have cleaned and released, only three—all murres—have been subsequently found again. One released off the Yorkshire coast of England was picked up six months later in Holland, still alive but with an injured leg. One released off the Yorkshire coast was picked up near the same spot (its home breed-ing ground) two years and one month later, having just died. A third released off the south coast of England and picked up in Eire two years and four months later was reoiled but still alive.

We must admit that from most batches of birds re-leased, there are almost invariably a small number that float in dead or dying within a few days, for which we have no explanation as yet. In spite of these failures, though, even a skeptic must concede that these examples do indicate that at least *some* of the birds survive.

From small pollution incidents we can put back to sea most of the birds received. In larger incidents the success rate drops to about 50 percent of those received, and while we confidently expect to improve on this performance, the number of birds saved from any major incident is likely to remain comparatively small in re-lation to the total number involved. That brings us to the third point of objection — is it worth doing at all? To answer this, we would quote Dr. C. M. Perrins in the Department of Zoology at Oxford University, writ-ing about auks on islands off the Welsh coast: "For species whose recruitment seems to be only marginally sufficient to replace the losses of breeding adults, even small reductions in such mortality might be critical if the populations are to survive."

Razorbill

The birds principally affected by oil spills at sea are the auks, members of which family include the murre, the razorbill and the puffin. Depending on where the spill occurs, other species, such as loons, sea ducks, grebes, gannets, etc., can also be affected, but nearly every incident includes auks, and they are usually the principal sufferers.

In addition to spills at sea, there are more than enough river and estuary incidents. In these, the principal vic-tims are swans and ducks, although a number of other species can be involved.

Mammals, notably seals, also can be caught up in oiling incidents, but there have been cases of otters being affected, and even sheep, though the involvement of mammals is usually minimal. Since birds are by far the greatest sufferers, this chapter will be devoted to them, but the *principles* of cleaning apply equally to any oiled mammal you may encounter. Obviously the actual *meth-*

Puffin

ods used to achieve the end result may need considerable modification to accommodate the species concerned. It would be rather difficult to get a large, irate bull seal into a bowl of water!

Possible Handling Hazards

The details in Chapters 1, 2 and 3 apply equally here. Obviously, if large numbers of birds are to be collected, it would be a sensible move to wear a pair of gloves both to protect the hands from bites and to save getting them covered in oil. Overalls and Wellington boots are a good idea, too.

Approach and Capture

In large-scale operations there will almost certainly be an organized team doing the collection, but it is by no means unusual for an individual bird to be found by an individual person, particularly after a bad storm. In this case the notes in Chapter 2 would apply; bear in mind that anything you cover the bird with may well be ruined by the oil.

Transportation

Contrary to what many people think, oiled birds can be carried for long distances with no apparent ill effects, provided they are not overcrowded and are carried in an enclosed vehicle. It is our contention that to a bird, standing in a moving vehicle is no different from standing in a static situation. It has no conception of "a vehicle" and consequently suffers no more stress from being in one than from being in any other situation outside its normal experience. We have received birds that have been on the road for periods up to ten hours, and the birds have arrived in much better condition than the drivers of the vehicles!

Cardboard pet carrier containers are ideal for auks, with no more than four in one which is roughly 18 × 12 × 12 inches. Other species such as ducks and divers can also be carried in these same boxes, but only one or possibly two to a box. Even gannets have been carried in the same sized boxes with no apparent ill effects, but we would recommend rather larger containers—cardboard boxes—for this large species.

After a great deal of experience we have dispensed with the practice of covering each bird with a poncho, or a covering with a hole for the head, having found that it can be dangerous to the birds and is of little value anyway. The idea was to prevent preening and consequent further ingestion of oil, but we have found that most sea birds do very little preening once they are out of sight of water, and the little they do is half-hearted and ineffectual. If an auk should fall over, as it is apt to do while wearing a poncho, it is usually quite unable to regain its feet and is consequently likely to be trampled on or fallen onto by the others. Tubular bandages and even socks have been used on occasion to immobilize birds totally, as well as to keep them warm. Such wrappings certainly achieve total immobilization, but we have found that far from keeping the birds warm, they appeared to have the effect of actually *lowering* the bird's body temperature. In incidents where birds have been sent to us wearing ponchos or other coverings, en route mortality has been over 20 percent; in incidents where they have been sent without such coverings, under 5 percent.

Initial Care

As well as depriving a bird of buoyancy, oil impairs the insulating qualities of the plumage, and since, for several reasons, most oiling incidents occur in the winter, the first essential is to provide a warm room in which to house the birds. Since they will, in all probability, have been without food for several days, a good meal is the second essential. We also begin as soon as possible after capture a short course of medication, which consists of Kaopectate, available at any pharmacy without prescription, dosage depending on species (refer to veterinarian).

The floor of the room or pen should be covered with thick newspaper or cloth, and this should be changed regularly to prevent further contamination with the bird's feces. Do *not* use hay, straw or similar covering (see "Symptoms, Diagnosis and Treatment" in this chapter, also Chapter 2, "Initial Care").

Food

The type of food offered obviously depends on the species involved, and for a guide to this, refer to the food sections of Chapters 1, 2 or 3.

Force-feeding

Most sea birds will accept food readily, if not from a dish, then thrown down in front of them. If your bird fails to eat, the best course is to slip it some food when administering its medication, although it should be noted that a sea bird that does not feed itself from the start seldom makes it back to sea (although you can keep such a bird alive in captivity virtually indefinitely). For methods of force-feeding, refer to the appropriate chapter for the species.

Symptoms, Diagnosis and Treatment

As mentioned in previous chapters, many wild birds and animals are infested with parasites, both internally and externally, and often infected by diseases that produce no symptoms unless the animal is under stress or physically below par.

Enteritis is another problem when the birds are first picked up. It may be caused by the stress, but it may also be caused, of course, by ingestion of oil. At any rate, as already described, the bird is treated with Kaopectate at the very beginning, and should enteritis flare up during the subsequent recovery period, further treatments may be given.

Aspergillosis has been found in many species of birds from different habitats, but mainly in temperate zones. The cause is a fungus which grows in the lungs and air sacs of the bird, and the symptoms produced when the disease is advanced are respiratory. The bird breathes with its beak open and produces a rattling sound. It is thought to be a major cause of death in herring gulls and mallards, and the source of infection is believed to be moldy food material and bedding, particularly hay and straw. Though it is a very common disease of penguins in captivity, no naturally occurring case has been found in wild penguins in the Antarctic. It is obviously a disease caused and certainly exacerbated by stress and overcrowding.

The common lesions found on postmortem examination are small, circumscribed yellow nodules varying from the size of a pinhead to a few centimeters in diameter. They are found in the lungs and air sacs, sometimes in the trachea and occasionally in other organs as well. The disease is spread by the spores, which are coughed up or excreted; these contaminate the food and can remain viable for a long period of time. Therefore, it is important to keep these wild birds on clean disinfected floors (such as concrete), on clean dry newspaper and in a building free from dust, cobwebs etc. Unfortunately to date there is no treatment for this disease.

Staphylococcal infection of the legs, which produces swaying of the joints and an inability to walk properly, is relatively common among wild birds that are kept on a hard floor for any length of time. This was particularly hazardous in the early days of treatment when birds were kept on concrete for long periods before being released. Nowadays the period of treatment has been very much reduced, and the birds can achieve a buoyant state in a much shorter time. This reduces the susceptibility to staphylococcal infection. Nevertheless, it does occur from time to time and can be arrested by treatment with a broad-spectrum antibiotic such as oxytetracycline. However, once it is well established in the bird, it is almost impossible to cure completely. Prevention, therefore, must be the main aim, and to this end keep the birds a minimum length of time in captivity and make sure that the areas where they are kept are as clean and sterile as possible. Newspapers, which are in plentiful supply, are unlikely to carry any infections and make an excellent floor covering—but replace them frequently.

General Care (Including Cleaning)

Although it is easy to describe how to clean birds, in practice it is a meticulous operation, and we do *not* recommend that people try it themselves. Knowing *how* to do it is not enough because a period of training is essential. In fact, we would say with virtual certainty that anyone trying it just from written instructions would have about as much chance of success as someone learning to drive a car by the same means.

Many processed oils are much more intractable than crude and are more difficult, or in some cases even impossible, to remove successfully. Heavy solvents should never be resorted to since the vapors exuded can kill the birds (rather defeating the object). Occasionally it may be necessary to retain birds for lengthy periods to let the oil simply weather off. This can be done with some species such as ducks or swans but should not be attempted with ocean species, such as auks, which become conditioned to human presence very easily. If these species are contaminated with a type of oil which does not yield to detergents, we would recommend they be destroyed. The only alternatives are to put them back to

sea less than adequately cleaned to face a lingering death
or to keep them permanently in captivity (see Appendix
A on the law).

When we receive oiled birds, we go about treatment
in the following way. We leave the bird to be cleaned
alone for about two or three days after its arrival—even
longer if it appears in poor condition. A fit bird has a
nice round, bright eye, and this is the most obvious
sign to look for in choosing a bird for cleaning.

A constant flow of water at high pressure and at 108°
F (42° C) is absolutely essential to the cleaning process.
*If this basic requirement is not available, there is no point
whatsoever in attempting to clean birds.* Other desirable
equipment includes a large sink, a supply of dishwashing
liquid (effective for most crude oils) and a room or pen
where the birds can be placed after cleaning, prior to
being moved out of doors. The water supply should be
equipped with a hand-held shower attachment, and there
should be two people to work as a team for each bird.

Make up a solution of dishwashing liquid in a bowl
of hot water 108° F (42° C) to a strength of about 2
percent (approximately half a cup to a large bowl of hot
water). The person holding should hold the bird in the
water up to its neck, and the person cleaning should
work the solution well into the plumage, paying particular attention to the head and neck. Dishwashing
liquid will do no harm to the eyes, and since the bird,
in subsequent preening, will rub the head over the rest
of the plumage, it is essential to clean the head as
thoroughly as any other part.

All the species normally involved in sea oiling incidents are capable of drawing blood with a bite, and this
can be quite painful on a hand softened by hot water.
The securing of the beak with a rubber band or similar
secure closing would be a judicious move. Take care not
to cover the nostrils of these species that have them. At
any sign of distress or vomiting the restraint must be
removed immediately; otherwise the bird may draw liquid into the lungs and quickly die.

When the solution has been well worked into the
head, back and tops of wings, the bird must be turned
over and the breast, flanks and underwings attended to.
Several changes of water and cleaning solution will be
necessary during this process, and the bird may need
more than one wash to remove all the oil, in which case

two or three days should elapse between sessions. Every trace of oil both on the surface and under the plumage must be removed. Most plumage can be vigorously agitated with no ill effects. Provided the center quill of a feather is not broken, the bird will "zip up" the disturbed barbs (the narrow strips to either side of the center quill forming the feather itself) quite easily, as well as rearrange the complete structure of the plumage, during subsequent preening. Gentleness is *not* synonymous with kindness in this operation.

When all the oil has been removed, the bird should be sprayed with the shower, again at 108° F (42° C); jet the water strongly into the plumage *against* the lay of the feathers so that it penetrates to the skin. This all-important part of the cleaning process should continue until the water beads off rather than soaks in, and this state must be achieved for the whole of the plumage. The water beads off when all the detergent has been removed, and the feathers return to their normal state.

It is a commonly held fallacy that when one washes a bird, the so-called natural oils are removed in the process, thereby denying the bird buoyancy. This is untrue. The secretion from the uropygial gland, or preen gland as it is usually called, has no bearing on buoyancy. Its function is now thought to pertain to feather *conditioning* and *insulation*. What does deny a bird buoyancy after washing is residues of the *cleaning agent* in or on the plumage; this has a similar effect to that of putting a finger on a tent when it is raining. What gives the bird its buoyancy is the substance of the feather (keratin, similar to a fingernail) plus the small pockets of air trapped between the barbs of each feather and in the structure of the plumage as a whole. In fact, what keeps the water out is the surface tension of the water itself. Putting a finger on a tent in the rain or leaving cleaning agent in or on a bird's plumage breaks this surface tension and allows the water to permeate. In the case of the tent there will merely be a steady drip at the point touched, but in the case of a bird the water will leak *under* the plumage at the point where the cleaner is left and so destroy the whole of the structure, which was not designed to resist water from the *inside*.

The spraying should be done systematically—head, neck, back, top of wings, then over for breast, flanks and underwings. During the rinsing operations the bird must be carefully held to ensure that detergent residues do not affect areas already cleaned. Once completely cleared of residues, the bird should be virtually dry, although the wings and tails of some species such as cormorants are not 100 percent waterproof and will remain wet after the cleaning process. If the job has been done properly, it should not be necessary to dry the bird, and it should not, at this stage, be wrapped in a cloth. Place the bird in a clean warm room or pen (obviously *not* the one it was using previously), and leave it alone to preen. Provide some food because most birds appear to be ready for a snack immediately after being cleaned. Do not, at this stage, use newspaper on the floor because the printer's ink may cause a bit of contamination of its own which was not obvious or critical before. Do not use cloth either; there is every likelihood it will contain residues of the detergent it was washed in, which may get onto the feathers.

Absorbent paper towels are ideal for the floor at this stage but may be prohibitive in price if a lot of birds are to be cared for, or end rolls of unused newsprint paper may be obtained from a local newspaper if you ask nicely; but if no clean paper is forthcoming, the floor may have to be left bare. The birds will be here for only one night, though, and should be able to go to an outside pool the following day. If the job has been done properly, *they should be completely buoyant*.

The outside paddock in which the birds are housed prior to release must be kept as clean as possible. For auks, smooth concrete is preferable. For others such as waterfowl, grass is satisfactory although this very quickly becomes contaminated with the bird's feces if the area is small. Whatever kind of pool is used, it must have its water changed and sediments cleaned out at least once a day. There should also be a facility for keeping up a constant flow, skimming the surface and preventing the build-up of a surface film on the water which may affect the bird's plumage, leading to a further loss of buoyancy.

Waterfowl need as much ground area as can be allocated, in addition to the pool. Auks need very little walking space, and their activities are best confined to a narrow ledge, no more than a foot wide, around the pool, which can be improvised in a number of ways — timber or concrete blocks covered with polythene sheeting, for instance. Auks also prefer a blank wall to stand against, as they do on cliff faces.

Do not put fish into the pool, for although it is nice to see the birds diving for them, oil from the fish contributes greatly to the build-up of a surface film in a small area.

Release

A buoyancy test must be carried out prior to release. The birds must be compelled to remain in the pool for a minimum of twenty minutes, by which time any deficiencies in their buoyancy will become apparent. It is not enough simply to observe the birds jumping in and out of the pool of their own volition, when they can look excellent and apparently perfect. Confinement to the water tells a different story, when water can slowly "leak" through even one small patch. The bird will begin to exhibit signs of this by spreading its wings on the surface and flapping in an endeavor to correct flotation level.

After the twenty-minute test each bird should be examined minutely and should be *completely dry* (except in the case of cormorants, mentioned earlier). If it passes this test and is also in good physical condition, it is ready to be released. *A bird should never be released if it has even a small damp patch, for it will most certainly perish.* In *optimum* circumstances, release can be as little as a week after capture. In practice, it usually works out a little longer, but release should be effected as soon as possible.

In oiling cases, it would be silly to take the birds back where they came from if there is a probability of oil still hanging around, and it is not necessary to do so. They can be released from any quiet stretch of coast. Any bird so released should be banded for future identification if possible.

PART TWO

MAMMALS

8

Small Ones

Norway rat

We are making a rather sweeping generalization here by lumping this group together in spite of their differences, as we did in Chapter 6. This time we are dealing with about 150 species, which might be something of an improvement on the 300 of Chapter 6.

The group ranges in size from the Norway rat (or common rat) and plains pocket gopher, which can be eighteen inches long, to the pigmy shrew, which comes in at about three inches plus one and a half inches of tail. Apart from moles and gophers, which have quite a distinctive appearance, the group bears a superficial resemblance to one another in that they all could be described as small furry animals—and this is about as much as many people would wish to know about them!

Most people would be able to identify a rat, brown or black, before they *and* the rat made a rapid departure from one another, but the others we deal with in this chapter are more difficult to tell apart. To the average city dweller, all small furry animals, if they aren't large enough to be rats, are mice, whereas there are in fact several groups. The shrews have very pointed muzzles, small ears that can hardly be seen and fairly short tails. Mice, too, have pointed muzzles (but nothing like as long as the shrews) but have ears which are fairly prominent and longish tails. The third group, the voles and lemmings, have inconspicuous ears and shortish tails (like the shrews) but blunt noses. The pikas, also in this group, look somewhat like tiny rabbits.

The odd ones out in the group are the moles and gophers, which have beautiful coats resembling velvet and front feet that appear to belong to a much larger animal. The fur of these animals is interesting in that it will lie in any direction—with most mammals it lies only pointing to the rear. The poor old mole is a creature

Mole

that suffers much more punishment than its crimes really warrant. Although we admit that it *looks* unsightly, most of the damage done by the offender is of a very superficial nature which, in a court of law, would call for a modest fine—not a prison sentence and certainly not the death sentence.

On the other hand, rats, both Norway and black, and the house mouse, if not kept under rigid control, could become strong rivals for very existence with the human race. They are overwhelmingly prolific and are sexually mature at a very early age (rats at three months, mice at only six weeks), producing anything up to thirty-five to forty young per year. Some simple mathematics will give an indication of just how breath-taking this recruitment rate is. They eat prodigious quantities of virtually anything edible and destroy much more by fouling. Rats in particular are very bright, not easily trapped, and they live anywhere and everywhere we do, doing extensive damage both to food supplies and to property.

Gopher

Although people in general are unaware of it, the human race is at constant war with these animals, and we aren't winning the war, only managing to hold our own. If we get down to basics, we are engaged in the same activity as every other species on earth—namely, the struggle for survival. We can live in peaceful co-existence with most species, but with some, tolerance and benevolence become luxuries which threaten our own species and, as such, simply cannot be afforded. Such a conflict of fundamental interests has always existed and will always exist between rats and house mice on the one hand and ourselves on the other.

As for the others in the group, shrews are harmless and indeed useful in that they eat snails and insects. The remainder *can* cause varying amounts of agricultural or forestry damage, depending on the density of a particular species in a particular area. In general, their numbers are kept in check by a variety of predators, including foxes, various birds of prey and weasels as well as domestic cats. Also, the life span of most is fleeting, by our standards, some as little as twelve to eighteen months.

Pigmy shrew

It is very seldom that a casualty of this group will come to hand since the principal cause of injury is attack by predators, and this is almost invariably fatal. As the reason for the attack is to provide a meal for said predator (or offspring), the carcasses are not left lying around, so it is seldom one comes across even a dead one. The only real exceptions to this are "things the cat dragged in," and even these, if still alive, are likely to be suffering severe shock and injuries from which they will not recover.

There are certain of the group—namely, rats and house mice—which we could not possibly recommend treating, even if anyone should wish to do so. There are points at which compassion becomes fanaticism, and this is one of them. It *is* possible to keep a rat or a house mouse as a pet. Domestic varieties of both are widely kept, although usually for experimental purposes, which is yet another subject and not part of this book. We do not recommend keeping one of the wild varieties as a pet since it would lead a life of utter frustration in such circumstances. Moles and shrews are brought to us occasionally after being caught by cats. Shrews frequently can be rescued from a cat still alive because although cats catch and kill these harmless and beneficial animals in large numbers, ironically they won't eat them. The only other casualties of the group we can recall from the past ten years or so are one vole and two harvest mice, and this probably reflects the public's feelings toward the group as a whole. As mentioned earlier, to most people all small furry creatures are mice (meaning house mice) and, as such, are more likely to be killed than rescued. Since this is our own view in the case of house mice, we can't really complain if a person who doesn't know the difference hits first and asks questions afterward. But it is a pity that the harmless ones suffer the same fate.

Vole

Possible Handling Hazards
Most of the group can, and will, bite, and apart from any injury caused by the bite itself, there may be other complications. The bite of the short-tailed shrew, one of the most common North American mammals and one of the most ferocious (at least so far as its prey is concerned), is poisonous, but although the venomous saliva paralyzes its victims, which mainly are small invertebrates, it is not dangerous to humans. However, the bite will prove quite painful for several days.

There is an amusing little animal in Britain that fits

into this group: the dormouse. The interesting thing about it is that it shows no inclination to bite at all. It is one of the very few "tame" wild animals, showing no fear of humans, and indeed exhibits only a friendly interest in anyone handling it. On one occasion a dormouse was brought in to us, and we could find nothing wrong with it. An assistant was instructed to take it out of harm's way, into one of the paddocks, where it could go or stay as it wished. The assistant returned a few moments later, having carried out the instructions, with the dormouse skipping along behind him!

Lemming

Approach and Capture
All members of this group are very agile and, in the open, very difficult to catch if still mobile. Even in a confined space their quick, darting movements are quite unpredictable. Trapping under a jam jar is about the best method of capture, and you can see through the glass just what it is you have caught—a mouse, a shrew or a vole. The exact species doesn't particularly matter at this stage. Obviously a rat or a gopher will not fit under a jam jar, and if one needs to be caught rather than killed, a coat should be thrown over it. It will prefer to stay under the coat in the dark than venture out in the open again. There are many reliably witnessed instances of rats attacking people, but the persons concerned are dead or incapacitated or are babies. The stories of cornered rats leaping for the throat of the person doing the cornering are somewhat more difficult to authenticate and are at best doubtful. In our experience, all of a rat's efforts are concentrated in trying to find a hiding place, with none left over for a counterattack on the pursuer. If you feel the slightest revulsion or fear, it is best you do not even attempt to catch a rat.

Transportation
If it should be necessary to transport the rat you have caught, wrap it up slowly and carefully in the coat you have covered it with; then drop it and the coat into a sack and tie the neck. The rat could, of course, chew its way out of these restraints quite easily but is not likely to do so while it can detect your immediate presence. A gopher, too, can be carried in this way.

With the others, if you have caught them under a jam jar, slide a piece of card under and turn the jar up the other way with the animal inside. Loosely fill the jar with shredded paper, and either replace the lid, punctured with air holes, or tie a piece of porous material over the top.

Initial Care

The black and Norway rats will now be left out of consideration, as will the house mouse, although the latter *could* be kept in the manner described hereafter, being of a similar size to the rest of the group.

Kangaroo rat

A chewproof container, such as an aquarium (without the water, of course), is required as a temporary residence, or failing anything else, a cookie or cracker tin will serve for the smaller members of the group. A smaller box in one corner filled with hay will be appreciated by most. This inner box can be of cardboard because it doesn't matter so much if it gets chewed. For a mole or gopher, half fill the aquarium or box with soil, and don't bother to provide the inner house since it will not be appreciated.

If using an aquarium, cover the top because several of the group are excellent at jumping. Whatever is used for the cover must, of course, have air holes, but these must be very tiny since some of these creatures can squeeze through amazingly small spaces. A piece of perforated zinc such as that used for meat safes is ideal for a cover, providing plenty of air through holes much too small for any escape. If you use a cookie can, the ordinary tin lid can form the cover with plenty of punctures made with a nail. Keep the aquarium/box in a fairly warm room unless the "client" is a jumping mouse that has been scratched out from hibernation (which could be anytime between October and April). In this case, place the box in a cool spot which is weather- and predatorproof, and leave it alone. It is preferable that the box, in this case, should have an exit for the animal to get out through as soon as it wakes up.

Food

Moles eat earthworms mainly, and in considerable numbers. They will accept a little dog food from time to time, simply left on the surface of the soil. In common with most of this group, the mole must eat frequently — at least every four hours day and night — in order to survive, so food must be available at all times.

Shrews eat mainly insects. They are partial to wood

lice and snails but will also accept small portions of any kind of meat, including the canned varieties.

Voles eat a wide variety of vegetable matter. They can be offered grain, cereals, apple, berries, vegetables (both root and leaf) and chick pellets. Lemmings, pikas and gophers are vegetarians and will accept one or more of the above items as well as sundry items such as grass, clover, buttercups, sunflower tubers, nuts, etc.

The many species of mice and rats eat a wide variety of things, and unless you are quite sure which species you are dealing with, it would be best to provide a variety of both vegetables and insects, as well as a little canned dog food, until you are able to observe the animal's preference. Remember, many of this group *must eat at frequent intervals, day and night*, so you haven't time to experiment with one thing at a time.

Water must be provided, although some drink very little, depending on the moisture content of the food being offered.

Force-feeding
Not a very practical proposition.

Symptoms, Diagnosis and Treatment
Injuries. Rarely, if ever, will a member of this group be found injured, for either the injuries are fatal or the animal will take itself and its injuries off as fast as possible.

Diseases and Poisoning. Not infrequently some species — usually rats and mice — may be found poisoned: semicomatose; lethargic; hunched up with disheveled coat. The poison most frequently used today is warfarin, which prevents blood from clotting, causing internal bleeding, and the animal takes a day or so to die.

Strychnine, the poison normally used to kill moles, is cruel, and in fact, its use on all animals except moles is forbidden. Because the baited earthworms are put down its tunnel, the horrible symptoms of periodic contraction of the muscles until the animal dies from asphyxia are not seen.

Voles, harvest mice and shrews may be poisoned by accident with mercury-treated grain used in planting or by agricultural pesticides, but one never sees a sick animal.

It is rare to come across a diseased mammal from this

group, but then you do not often see a healthy one either in the garden or countryside. But as with all the other wild creatures, disease is a hazard to which many succumb. Rats get a type of typhoid with the general name of salmonella, and some types are infectious to humans. Rats are also susceptible to infectious anemia and to leptospirosis, which can affect dogs as well as humans. Brucellosis, too, has infected rats, as have a number of other diseases. Perhaps their susceptibility to so many diseases explains why they are often used as experimental animals.

Mice are almost as vulnerable as rats, and the spread of disease is enhanced by numbers living close together. Less is known about voles and shrews, though they seem to be susceptible to fewer diseases. Moles have apparently not attracted the attention of the scientists researching disease, for there are few reports in the literature.

As may be expected, all small mammals are susceptible to both ecto- and endoparasites (external and internal parasites). Ticks, mites, fleas and lice all infect this group of small mammals quite commonly. It will be remembered that bubonic plague—the Black Death which killed millions in Europe during the lifetime of Newton—was spread by fleas to both rats and human beings.

If ectoparasites did not spread disease, they would be no more than a nuisance to the host. But fleas are responsible for spreading several diseases, including a tapeworm that is common in mice, with the flea acting as its intermediate host. For this reason, some rescuers may wish to dust the animal with a powder to get rid of them. They are not, however, dangerous to human beings. Ticks are much more difficult to deal with, and fortunately they do little harm. Their mouthparts are so embedded in the skin of their host that pulling on the body will tear the tick apart, leaving the mouthparts in the skin, where they sometimes cause irritation and suppuration. A drop of ether or chloroform onto the tick will make it let go and fall off. Alcohol may work, too.

General Care
The animal should be housed and cared for as outlined in "Initial Care" until ready for release. There is no

advantage to be gained from putting it out of doors, and such a course may well prove detrimental unless it is placed well in the shade.

Release

In the case of a water shrew or water vole, take the animal to the vicinity of a stream for release. For the rest, simply place the sleeping box under a hedge away from a road. In the case of a jumping mouse you have been wintering, make sure the animal is fully awake. Although some of the group can be seen during the day, it is best to effect a release just before dark.

Orphans

We have never reared the orphans of any of this group, and it is unlikely you will ever be called upon to do so — just as well since we would not rate your chances of success very highly.

Earlier mention of the prodigious reproductive rate of some of this group reminds us of the small boy who arrived one day bearing a cardboard box. "Could you find a new home for this mice?" he asked.

We opened the box to find a solitary white mouse. We promised to do our best and later had a good laugh at the boy's use of the plural instead of the singular.

As happens all too often, however, the laugh was on us — for the next day the mouse produced a family of six!

9

Bats

In a contest to find the animal that makes people cringe most, the bat must surely rate very high—certainly in the first three alongside snakes and spiders. Bram Stoker and authors of that ilk bear much of the blame with their tales of vampires, but it must be admitted that the bats themselves do not present a very attractive appearance to the average human eye; that is, of course, no fault of theirs. Another factor which doesn't help their popularity is their association in most people's minds with belfries and graveyards, though they can be found in a wide variety of locations. We recently came across a colony living in the roof space of a new house on a large estate, much to the horror of the tenant, who thought it a reflection on her household cleanliness (like having cockroaches in the kitchen, which, incidentally, is also erroneous; see Chapter 21).

Big-eared bat

The vast majority of people have never seen a bat close up—the usual view is of shadowy forms flitting about in the twilight as they catch their evening meal—but most people can identify one, although they would probably have no idea which of the native species it might be.

In America bats vary from the solitary, such as the silver-haired, to those living in very large groups. The Brazilian free-tailed bat, for instance, is quite a tourist attraction in the Carlsbad Caverns of New Mexico, as vast numbers emerge in the evening and return in the morning, numbering some hundreds of thousands.

In flight, a bat's incomparable skill and maneuverability make the average bird look like a rank amateur. Bats stop, turn at right angles in midair, change direction in seemingly impossible ways, and of course, they have the added refinement of built-in echo location systems which virtually eliminate the danger of collisions with any obstacle. (Thus you can disabuse yourself of the ridiculous notion that a bat might entangle itself in your hair.) We recently heard a story of a rare collision, but inasmuch as it was with a fishing line at twilight, the bat can't really be blamed! The person concerned—a girl with long hair—was rather surprised after her inexpert cast to feel tugging in the sky rather than in the river and to find she'd hooked a bat instead of a plump salmon. She wound the line in, the bat hung confidently from her finger while she gently detached the hook from the wing membrane and then it flew off happily into the air. A variation on the one that got away!

Of the thirty-nine species recorded in the United States, the largest is only about seven and a half inches long, and even this "monster" is quite rare. An average of the large ones is about four to six inches, and it can do no harm: they all are completely inoffensive creatures, which will harm neither humans nor their property, even if they *are* squatting in the roof space.

Leaf-nosed bat

Since bats really have no enemies, one would expect them to be very numerous except that they usually give birth to only one infant each year. The baby is hairless and helpless, but it can grab hold of and cling to its mother, who carries it about when she flies out feeding. After a time, however, it gets too big, and she will leave it "hanging about" while she goes out and will suckle it when she gets back. By the time the baby is seven weeks old it can fly.

Some American species hibernate in the winter, while others migrate south to warmer climates up to 1,000 miles away. Hibernating species choose places with very particular climatic conditions: There must be ventilation but no drafts, and the moisture content must not be too low. Favorites for the purpose are caves, most of which have very steady temperature and humidity (as our ancestors found!). Hibernating bats will die if their immediate temperature drops below freezing.

Possible Handling Hazards

Some species are quite amenable to being handled and do not seem to be bothered at all, while others will bite and some can draw blood. We hasten to add, before the mention of blood reconjures thoughts of vampires, that

Free-tailed bat

they will bite only when you catch hold of them — they will not attack, and they will not lap up the blood their bite might cause! They are susceptible to rabies, and unlike other animals, they often recover, meaning they could possibly be carriers, and even though this is thought not to be the case, take care to avoid the possibility of a bite in handling. By the way, even the spine-chilling vampire (which you are unlikely to encounter anyway) does not normally attack humans but contents itself with sucking the blood of birds and, less frequently, cattle, pigs and horses, among which it occasionally has spread rabies (see Chapter 16 for more about rabies).

Approach and Capture
It is quite simple to catch perfectly fit bats, should it be necessary for purposes of relocation (see "General Care"). If you can manage to get into their roosting place, they can just be picked off their perch.

Some bats have difficulty in getting into the air when grounded and require only a lift onto a ledge or tree branch.

Transportation
A dark box is of the essence should you need to transport bats. A cardboard one will be quite adequate, and in it you should firmly wedge a piece of rough timber to which the bats can cling in their normal upside-down posture. They will be much more at ease if offered this simple facility than if just left to crawl on the bottom of the box.

Initial Care
Bats seldom become genuine casualties, and on the comparatively rare occasions we cared for a bat — never for more than one or two days — we have kept it in a box as above with a suitable piece of timber to cling to.

Food
Dried flies (obtainable from pet stores) dampened in a little water appear to be acceptable, but again we cannot claim any great experience on which to base a sound judgment. They have certainly been eaten by one or two of the bats we have kept. A little canned dog food could be tried, too, should a bat have to be kept for some time.

Symptoms, Diagnosis and Treatment

The only injury we have ever come across in bats is a torn wing membrane, and even this is rather rare because of the animal's great flying skill. A torn membrane can be sutured, using fine nylon thread, provided the tear is not too great. The skin or membrane between the elongated fingers is well supplied with blood, and if the edges are brought together accurately, it should heal fairly well.

See earlier reference to rabies, also Chapter 16.

General Care

We are sorry to offer so little information in the foregoing sections on the care of bats in captivity, but there is little point in airing knowledge which you don't possess. Since we have nothing to add regarding general care in captivity, we thought a few notes on helping to care for bats in the wild might not come amiss.

Buildings are used extensively by a number of species, and it is here they are likely to come into conflict with people, even though bats confine their activities normally to those parts of buildings not being used by human residents, such as roof spaces, wall cavities or indeed any place which offers good shelter but is reasonably "private."

It is fair to say that they are good neighbors. They do not make a lot of noise (at least not that you can hear), do not make nests or damage the building in any way; their droppings are dry and very nearly odorless and do not have any of the corrosive qualities of bird droppings. They are clean and prefer to live in a clean environment, and last but not least, they are night-shift workers, so they don't bother you at all during the day. In fact, all they do is mind their own business, which in no way intrudes on that of the other residents of the building. They are so unobtrusive that very often people are unaware they are on the premises. In addition to being good neighbors, they consume thousands of tons of assorted insect pests—a boon to the farmer and gardener.

That having been said, all the begging, pleading and cajoling you can muster will not persuade some people, who flatly refuse to tolerate bats in their house. On one occasion a chap turned up with a box containing thirty-seven which he'd been obliged to remove from his roof space. His wife had left the house as soon as she learned they were there and refused to enter again until the poor old bats were forcibly ejected! Such extreme cases are rare, fortunately, since removal in this manner is not a good idea. Most people who want to get rid of bats are prepared to "serve notice to quit" and allow a reasonable time for the eviction to be executed. The procedure recommended by the British Royal Society for Nature Conservation is the best one to follow, and we quote from its interesting leaflet *Focus on Bats*.

The whereabouts of exit holes and the approximate number of bats present should be ascertained by watching on two consecutive evenings from sunset to darkness. During the next day, little-used holes should be sealed with appropriate materials, leaving the main exit open. The same evening, bats should be counted again whilst they are emerging to forage and when all appear to have left, rags should be pushed firmly into the hole preventing their return. Early the following evening, the rags should be removed so as to allow any further bats to escape before finally filling the hole.

If this method is adopted, *two important precautions* must be taken to ensure that dead rotting bodies are not left in the building causing smell and damage. First, no action be taken between mid-June and about the 20th of August because young bats remain in the roof when mother leaves to feed. Secondly, avoid action during cold weather because none or only a few bats will emerge to feed each evening.

10

Hares and Rabbits

The rabbit is probably the most familiar of all wild mammals. Apart from the agricultural community, which places it low in the popularity stakes, it is familiar to and loved by most of us—reared as we are on a diet of endearing characters such as Peter Rabbit and that most debonair cartoon personality Bugs Bunny, delightful little Easter bunnies decorating shop windows and, in recent years, the splendid cast of Richard Adams's *Watership Down.* Rabbits have also been kept as domestic pets for a long time and are now to be found in all shapes and sizes, so people generally feel closer to the rabbit than to other wild mammals.

Many look upon the wild population, too, as "pets" and wouldn't hesitate to pick one up. Even its severest critics could not deny the rabbit's winsome appearance with those outsize ears and back feet, that perky expression and hopping gait, brought up at the rear with that little white powder puff of a tail. There is little wonder it has been anthropomorphized out of all recognition.

In North America there are eight species of hare, of which the white-tailed and black-tailed jack rabbits are by far the most common. Of rabbits proper, there are also eight species, nine, if you count the European, which has been introduced in several places, usually with disastrous results, as in the case of its introduction to San Juan Island, Washington.

It should be explained that the European rabbit is an expert digger, excavating tunnels like nobody's business! The lighthouse keeper of San Juan Island didn't quite appreciate this fact when he imported a few to supplement the fresh meat supply, and it wasn't until the lighthouse was on the verge of collapse from the tunneling activities of thousands of rabbits that the situation was brought under control.

There is much interesting fact and folklore about hares. For instance, they are reputed to be able to run faster up a hill than down and to lead any pursuer purposely up a hill, should there be one in the vicinity, where they can demonstrate their superiority. The antics of the "mad March hare" are a joy to watch should you ever chance to view the spectacle. They aren't really mad, of course—the leaping about and sparring with each other only *look* mad to us. It is mating behavior and doubtless very serious to the hares!

Hares and rabbits belong to the same family of animals and look very much alike. Yet from the point of view of caring for them in captivity, there is one very significant difference (see "Orphans"). There are many other physical differences between hares and rabbits, but the easiest one to remember is that most hares have black tips to the ears (even the northern in its winter coat) and rabbits do not. Also, apart from the European rabbit, hares are generally larger than rabbits and, having longer, more powerful legs, tend to live in the open and rely on speed to escape predators.

Possible Handling Hazards
Many people unhesitatingly pick up a hare or rabbit, never dreaming that there could be any danger from a "bunny." In the majority of cases this is right, but both the rabbit and the hare can, and sometimes do, bite, and the bite can be quite severe. They frequently cause painful scratches with the hind feet. Although this is by accident in an attempt to escape rather than by design, it doesn't lessen the pain!

Approach and Capture
If one of this group is still mobile, your chances of catching it are virtually nil. It is only when the injury is incapacitating that there is any chance of approaching the animal. There is an old theory, though, that you can come right up to a perfectly fit hare by walking around it in decreasing circles, and we tested it once on a hare that was sitting virtually in the middle of a three-acre meadow. The walker started with a very wide circle and approached the hare slowly but quite steadily, not looking at the animal directly, until no more than twelve feet separated the walker from the "subject." At that point the hare decided it had seen enough of this idiot

Jack rabbit

wandering around in circles and bolted, proving, however, that there was some truth in the theory.

On being approached, an injured animal will frequently give a piercing scream of sheer terror which can be a bit unnerving if you haven't heard it before. Doing all the handling slowly and gently with no sudden movements will do much to calm this terror.

It is quite in order for one hand to hold the ears—indeed, it is the best way to avoid being bitten—but the other hand *must* support the weight of the body when lifting. A rabbit or hare should never be lifted by the ears alone. Place the supporting hand so that you avoid scratches to the forearm from the hind feet. Under the rump is the best position.

Transportation
A member of this group will appreciate being in the dark, and a stout cardboard box will serve for a short journey. Although a fit hare or rabbit could very easily demolish such a container, one that is injured is likely to be grateful for the seclusion. Don't forget to provide a few air holes. For longer journeys and those where you cannot keep an eye on the container during the trip, a wicker car basket is ideal. Cover it with a coat or something to make it darker inside, but be sure ample air can get in.

Initial Care
The animal will most appreciate being left alone in a quiet place with a soft bed of hay or straw to recover from the initial trauma of the injury and the capture and handling. Place within reach a handful of grass, clover and/or apple along with a shallow bowl of water, water, and leave the patient overnight unless there is some wound requiring immediate attention. There should normally be no need to provide artificial heat for an adult member of this group, and it may even be detrimental to do so.

Food
Hares and rabbits are easy to feed, especially during the summer months. Give them grass, clover, dandelion, carrot and turnip tops, cabbage, grain, cereals or apple, and if hay is provided for bedding, they are also likely to consume some of this.

Water should always be available. Serve it in the

heaviest bowl you have because members of this group always seem curious to see what is under a bowl and are likely to turn it over.

It is natural and necessary for hares and rabbits to eat some of their own feces, for this is part of their digestive process.

Force-feeding

Not recommended. If your patient cannot feed itself, its chances of survival are very small, and it is unlikely to be helped by attempted force-feeding.

Symptoms, Diagnosis and Treatment

Injuries. Road accidents are the usual causes of injury to rabbits, and more often than not one or more legs are broken. If the injuries are extensive, it may be kinder to put the animal to sleep. Occasionally one may be found entangled in a snare, and again, if a limb is badly damaged or there is a great loss of skin, it may be a kindness to put the animal to sleep. Sometimes a young rabbit may be carried home by a dog or a cat, or during a country walk you may surprise a weasel that has just caught a young rabbit. In these cases the animal is often so shocked that there is little chance of recovery, but this is not always the case.

Cottontail

The minor wounds can be treated at home in the usual way, but major lacerations and broken legs are best taken to the veterinarian.

Diseases. Rabbits and hares are susceptible, like most animals, to a variety of diseases, most of which are not easily recognized by the layperson. Perhaps the most important is a plaguelike disease called tularemia which normally affects lagomorphs (rabbits and hares) and rodents but which has been diagnosed in many other species, including humans. It causes an acute fever that often terminates in the death of the animal, and it is spread by blood-sucking parasites, such as fleas, flies, lice and ticks.

One other disease is worth mentioning—namely, Rocky Mountain spotted fever, which is now commonly recognized outside the Rocky Mountain area. It is a distressing disease in humans, beginning with a severe headache and illness three to seven days after infection from the bite of an infected tick; recovery is slow. The several species of ticks that can carry the disease are normally found on a few species of wildlife, usually rabbits, hares and rodents, and sometimes in large numbers — one report claims to have found 17,000 ticks on a snowshoe hare and large numbers on cottontail rabbits.

Fibromatosis, a virus disease spread by blood-sucking insects, affects both rabbits and hares, causing first an inflammation and then dark lumps, often called horns by hunters, that can reach an inch in diameter. Young animals are more susceptible, and the lump persists much longer in them. In hares the lumps are most frequently found at the base of the ears and on the legs and eyelids. Eventually they regress.

Myxomatosis, a South American virus disease of rabbits, was first diagnosed outside South America, in San Diego, California, in 1930. Soon after, in Australia, scientists set about increasing the virulence of myxomatosis virus. Australia was overrun by rabbits because, having been introduced by humans, they had no natural enemies. Finally the virus was released in 1950, and it spread like wildfire, killing well over 90 percent of Australia's rabbits. Vast areas of the land began to become green again. A French farmer immediately realized its potential and in 1952, brought it to France, where again it spread rapidly. Then, in 1953, a British farmer brought it to England, where the rabbit population had reached almost 100 million! The population crashed to 250,000 or less because 90 percent of infected rabbits die. As with the other virus diseases mentioned, the virus is spread by a blood-sucking insect — in England by the rabbit flea.

Rabbits are also affected by parasites, both coccidiosis and worms, but are rarely found in the diseased state, and the public is unlikely to have to diagnose or treat these conditions.

General Care

Any outdoor enclosure should have the added refinement of wire netting on the base; otherwise your patient is very likely to indulge in a bit of excavation during the night. The outside pen need not be very tall. The easiest type to construct is one of triangular shape (on the end) with a simple covered section at one end and the rest covered in wire netting (see fig. 9, page 44). Two-inch mesh is best for the base, allowing grass to poke through, and the pen can be moved to a new position each day. This assumes you have an area of grass, but if you haven't, the animal should still be moved out of doors as soon as possible, even if the pen has to be placed on concrete.

If the pen is on grass, there is no need to provide anything more elaborate by way of a house than the simple shelter illustrated. Bear in mind that although they look like them, these are *not* domestic pets (which require more cosseting for a happy life).

Release
Do not keep the animal penned up longer than absolutely necessary. As soon as it is reasonably fit and able to move at speed, let it out to take its chances, and its best chance will be as far away as possible from arable farmland.

Orphans
It is with the young that the major difference between hares and rabbits lies, and it is quite a startling difference. Baby rabbits are born blind, deaf, virtually bald and incapable of movement, whereas baby hares (leverets) are born fully developed with eyes open and capable of hopping about virtually from birth. Leverets are very near to the storybook images of the "Easter bunny."

When you deal with young, it must be remembered that a newborn leveret resembles a rabbit that is nearly three weeks old and is not far from being able to exist independently (as both can do at about four weeks). Consequently the leveret appears to need bottle feeding much longer than the rabbit. For bottle feeding use a half milk, half water mixture with an added pinch of glucose. Five or six feedings a day is adequate, and feeding during the night is not necessary. Each youngster will take anything from one-fifth to one-third ounce per feeding. Watch for the mouth filling up and *remaining* full, which is an indication that the youngster has had enough. A plastic syringe is the best feeding bottle.

By about the middle of the third week baby rabbits will be starting to nibble food, leverets sometimes earlier, but both should still be bottle-fed, with the number of feedings being reduced as the intake of solids increases. Both should be quite finished and on a completely adult diet by the end of the fourth week. It will do no harm to put down a dish of milk for them to drink for a further week. Ideally the "nursery" should consist of a long wooden box with solid sides to keep out drafts. The floor can be covered with sawdust, wood shavings or thick newspaper, and at one end make a nest of hay or shredded paper tissues. Provide a bit of warmth around the nest area in the early days, particularly for baby rabbits, but do not make it too hot. Around 68° F (20° C) is adequate. An infrared dull emitter is best, but an ordinary red electric light bulb, as used in electric fires, will do. The bedding should be kept dry, and this may mean a complete change every day, depending on the number of youngsters in the nest.

Turn off any artificial heat after two weeks, and move the youngsters out of doors as soon as possible after they have been weaned. The type of pen suggested for adult casualties will suit youngsters equally well, but baby rabbits in particular are rather slippery customers and will squeeze through anything their heads will fit. They will easily get through two-inch mesh netting, so one-inch mesh is advised.

Do not keep the youngsters any longer than is absolutely necessary to ensure complete self-sufficiency, and effect release in the manner suggested for adult casualties.

By the way, baby hares are much easier to rear than baby rabbits, which can, and frequently do, die in spite of the very best care.

11

Squirrels

The United States is particularly well endowed with members of this group; a view with which many farmers would doubtless ruefully agree. In the squirrel family there are no fewer than sixty-three species, varying widely in size, appearance and habits. Say "squirrels" to most people, and they will immediately think of tree squirrels and possibly chipmunks, some of which are common in urban areas but ground squirrels, prairie dogs and marmots (including the woodchuck) all are members of the squirrel family.

If asked to choose, the chipmunks, with their alert, inquisitive bearing and their handsome striped coats, busily stuffing their cheek pouches with stores for the winter hibernation, would probably be our favorites in the group.

Tree squirrels are also alert and quick movers. Most common is the gray, which is active all year, searching for its stores because it has forgotten where it has hidden them. It can also be quite impudent. One of our acquaintance persistently climbed into a house through an upstairs bathroom window—which it could reach only by negotiating a perilous series of drainpipes and gutters—to sprawl out for a nap on the fluffy shag cover of the toilet seat! The principal feature of the tree squirrel is its large, bushy tail.

Chipmunk

Ground squirrels have only moderate tails and are more like prairie dogs in general appearance as well as in habits, being ground dwellers and burrowers. The black-tailed prairie dog is surely the burrower par excellence, living in vast subterranean "towns" that cover many acres and contain several thousand animals. Like its human counterpart, the town is divided into separate districts, or wards, which in turn have a number of separate family groups or coteries.

One would think that in such a large community, there would be problems of inbreeding. Not so. The prairie dog has this all worked out. Females go to another coterie just to be mated, refusing to mate with genetic relations, and return to their home coterie immediately. A female will guard her pups jealously, but even so, in about 30 percent of cases another female will kill any undefended pups she finds. There is no doubt that this phenomenon contributes to stabilizing the population.

Prairie dog

Alongside some of the smallest chipmunks, some weighing as little as one ounce, the marmots are positive monsters, weighing in at fifteen pounds or so and in appearance, looking like outsize ground squirrels.

Possible Handling Hazards

As with hares and rabbits, appearances can be deceiving, and a set of teeth like well-honed chisels is concealed behind that jaunty, friendly demeanor. Squirrels are not averse to biting when circumstances warrant, such as when some well-meaning person is trying to take hold of them. They can inflict a substantial injury or injuries which could well need a few stitches.

Approach and Capture

Most of the group, even injured ones which are still mobile, are fast-moving and agile, with the added ability in many of being able to shin rapidly up trees and even rough walls. Short of employing elaborate netting, there is little chance of a successful capture, and even with the aid of nets, there is every likelihood the squirrel will still make you look like a fool. In approaching one that is apparently incapacitated, it is a good idea to get between the animal and any tree or wall it might still be able to scale in spite of its injury. In the case of ground dwellers try to get between the animal and its burrow, although it must be added that this possibility is extremely unlikely unless the animal is completely incapacitated.

A *very strong* glove, preferably a gauntlet, is recommended for picking up the smaller group members. Otherwise have the open traveling container very near at hand, pick up the animal by the tail and deposit it quickly into the container. It is possible to do this without damage to the animal and with no apparent

Gray squirrel

pain because most squirrels weigh very little, but the maneuver must be completed quickly, before the animal begins to struggle. Obviously a marmot is too heavy to be treated in this way, and two strong gloves or a dog grasper are recommended (see Chapter 13).

Transportation

A healthy squirrel can easily chew its way out of a wooden box, but such a container should last the trip home with an injured one. For a journey of any great length, some kind of metal box would be preferable; remember, of course, to puncture plenty of air holes in it. Tree squirrels are not happy about being shut in a completely closed box, so don't keep the animal confined any longer than absolutely necessary.

*Ground
squirrel*

A marmot will usually travel quite happily in a wooden crate of adequate size.

Initial Care

An indication has already been given of this group's prowess at demolishing timber, so do not simply shut one in a room of your house and expect the fixtures and fittings to remain intact, even if the patient appears to be totally incapacitated. Equally, there is not much point in shutting it in a garden shed unless the shed is constructed of brick or concrete block or something equally gnawproof.

In the early stages you really cannot do better than an ordinary birdcage. It does not have the claustrophobic effect of a closed box, and at the same time it can be partially covered with a cloth to offer a measure of seclusion. Don't cover it with one of your best tablecloths, or the squirrel is sure to pull it through the bars and tear it to ribbons. An old cloth that you don't want will probably be left alone! Cover the floor of the cage with sawdust preferably, but newspaper will do. Provide some food and water; then leave the patient alone pending examination.

Needless to say, a marmot would not take too kindly to being stuffed into a birdcage, and your garden shed may be the only place for it.

Food

Nuts rank high in popularity with most of the squirrel species. Ordinary peanuts will do nicely, with or without the shells, but not salted. In addition, a wide variety of other things will be accepted and devoured with evident relish. In the army, when someone eats and apparently enjoys anything and everything placed before him, they say he is "a good man at the trough." A squirrel could fairly be described thus, for it never turns up its nose at anything. Greens, vegetables, fruit, cereals, chick pellets, even the occasional cracker and jam or peanut butter sandwich! Nuts should be offered every day with other things on the list as and when available.

Force-feeding

A squirrel, even an injured one, will normally eat quite readily in captivity, so if it doesn't, there is something preventing it, and that something will almost certainly be serious enough to warrant the decision to destroy the animal. Force-feeding is not recommended both for this reason and for the hazard to the hands of the feeder. *Squirrel bites are not to be underestimated.*

Flying squirrel

Symptoms, Diagnosis and Treatment

Injuries. Few animals from this group are found injured. Perhaps the most common injury is caused by being hit by a car, and this is infrequent, or being caught in a steel-jawed trap, which usually causes death. Unless the injury is slight, it is best to take the animal to a veterinarian for treatment or to be put to sleep.

Diseases and Poisoning. Squirrels are susceptible to diseases, some of which have not yet been diagnosed. Tularemia and Rocky Mountain spotted fever, already mentioned in the chapter on rabbits, also affect squirrels.

The fibromatosis virus which affects squirrels is not the same as that affecting hares and rabbits. But the lesions look similar. The tumors are scattered over all the body and range in size from a pinhead to a half inch or an inch in diameter. The virus causing this disease is probably spread by mosquitoes. There is no treatment.

It is improbable, however, that a member of the public will ever find a live diseased squirrel. What you may find, however, is a sickly or dead animal in an area where poison has been laid to reduce their numbers, where they are causing damage to trees. The drug often used is an anticoagulant, which causes internal bleeding. There is no treatment, and the animal should be put to sleep.

General Care

A squirrel could undoubtedly chew a hole in the ordinary lightweight wire netting normally used for garden aviaries, for its gnawing abilities, especially through wood, are prodigious. But we have never seen any of our squirrel "clients" even attempt to bite wire. It's unlikely the squirrels are aware this particular barrier is too strong for them; more likely it's that chewing wire in order to effect an escape simply has no appeal. The aviary in which we have always housed squirrels is made of one-inch mesh chain link (apparently no longer available), and this has always proved entirely secure. If an outside pen is to be specially constructed, use strong wire mesh welded at each intersection, which comes in a wide variety of mesh sizes and wire thicknesses. Be sure to use the rigid kind rather than ordinary wire netting. A one-inch mesh with a wire thickness of 16 gauge would be suitable for squirrels and would also double as an aviary for a wide variety of birds.

It is quite safe to house a squirrel in an aviary containing birds of the crow family, pigeons, pheasants, etc., as well as rabbits and guinea pigs. There may be a bit of initial chasing around, but there is little likelihood of harm to either side. It may even be safe to house a squirrel with smaller birds, but not having tried this, we cannot recommend it.

It is generally accepted that some squirrels will take birds' eggs and even nestlings, but we housed one particular gray squirrel in an aviary where pigeons regularly laid eggs, and the squirrel took no interest in them whatsoever. Nor did it attempt to harm any squeakers (baby pigeons). It even occupied the top compartment of a pigeon cote within the aviary, with pigeons and jackdaws occupying the rest!

A small wooden box about a foot square will be readily adopted as a den by most of the smaller species. It should be fastened on the side of a wire pen for the climbers or simply left on the ground for the "landlubbers." Obviously a proportionally larger box is required for the larger species.

It is best to let the squirrel itself do the furnishing. Throw a couple of handfuls of hay on the ground, and the squirrel will collect it and carry it to the den. Incidentally, it appears to prefer two entrances to its residence, and if you provide only one, the squirrel is likely to chew out another one itself.

It is preferable that at least part of the ground area should be grass. Some of the group will indulge in digging and are very good at it, so provision must be made under the grass to forestall this with wire mesh or concrete blocks. The grass area provides somewhere to bury stores. The squirrel does this by carefully parting the topsoil to both sides while holding the nut in its mouth; the nut will then be placed in the small hole, and the topsoil rapidly but carefully patted back in place.

Release

Some of the group hibernate, and some don't. Some even hibernate in the summer (estivate). Consult a good reference book, such as *The Audubon Society Field Guide*, for the habits of the particular species you have been caring for, for the right time of year to release and the best location.

Squirrels, especially gray, are very unpopular with foresters, and there is no doubt they do considerable damage, particularly to very young trees. If and when you are releasing a squirrel, try to do so in an old woodland as far away from inhabited or tilled land as possible.

Orphans

The felling of a tree containing a nursery den may well produce squirrel infants in need of care and rearing. Older babies, not yet adept at the art of climbing, frequently fall out of trees, and these should be left alone, for the mother will almost certainly be along to attend to them. Ground-dwelling species of this group are much less likely to be found as infants young enough to require bottle feeding.

Baby squirrels adapt readily to a human foster parent, even from their very early days, when they are blind and naked.

The first essential is the provision of a warm, snug artificial den—a high-sided cardboard or wooden box which will keep out the drafts or even a large plastic plant pot. You will want to place the den substitute inside a cage when the babies start to move around, so bear this in mind when you choose the size of your den. For bedding, put in plenty of tissues or, better still, a generous amount of the new type of pet bedding, made of finely shredded paper, sold by most pet stores. Artificial heat should be provided to keep the den at about 86° F (30° C) constant.

Initial feeding should be on the same mixture and at the same rate as for baby rabbits (Chapter 10, page 101) but will need to be continued for at least five weeks, which is about two weeks after the eyes open, and thereafter until they can feed themselves properly at about eight weeks. About a week after the eyes open is the time to start offering a little more solid food. As you lift each one out for a feeding, have a shallow dish of bread and diluted warm milk handy, and offer it *before* giving the "bottle." At first there will be little response, but if the youngsters have been brought in very young and have consequently been hand-fed for quite some time, they will associate being lifted out of the den with having food. If this is withheld for a few moments and the youngster's mouth is steered in the direction of the dish, it will soon get the idea. The bottle feeding must continue as indicated above.

As soon as the youngsters show interest in coming out of the den of their own accord, it is time to move them (and the den) into a cage but still indoors. There should, by this time, be no need to continue the artificial heating, but keep the cage up off the floor in case of drafts. Obviously the larger the cage, the better, and a close-meshed parrot cage is ideal. Put at least one piece of tree branch in for climbing practice.

Continue to provide the bread and milk which was their first introduction to solid food, but begin to introduce other things. Pieces of apple and chick pellets are good starters, as are nuts, of course, but these should be shelled first. A dish of water should also be provided and remain at all times.

When they are feeding themselves entirely, they can be moved out of doors, at which time they can be provided with conditions similar to those for adult casualties. Put some bedding in the sleeping box for them, though, because they won't quite have the knack of collecting their own at this stage.

Allow at least a further month before final release or until winter is over if you find them late in the year, and effect the release as for adult casualties.

12

Weasels (and Similar)

Seven species are featured in this chapter. In size order, starting with the smallest, they are the least weasel (at about seven inches long), long-tailed weasel, ermine, black-footed ferret, mink, marten and fisher (at up to forty inches). An elongated body is the principal feature, together with rather short legs. For our money, the handsomest of the group, as well as the rarest, is the black-footed ferret with its distinctive Lone Ranger mask!

Black-footed ferret

It would be true to say that extensive trapping has by no means helped this group. The poor old ermine, for instance, has been called upon to sacrifice its coat in order to trim the robes of lords and ladies and dignitaries for many years. We are inclined to think it looks better on the animal.

As well as being trapped for fur, the group suffers great persecution from gamekeepers and poultry farmers. Actually, however, these animals can be only beneficial to the rest of the farming community and foresters since they kill rabbits and a great many rodents. The marten also disposes of squirrels, pleasing the foresters.

It is always difficult to plead the case for continuing existence of an animal that people seldom, if ever, see. "If we never see it," they might say, "what difference does it make if it isn't there at all?" From a purely aesthetic point of view, there is no answer to this. You can't see any less of an animal that becomes extinct if you never saw it when it existed! But ecologically there is always a difference. When a species is wiped out, it could lead to the decimation or proliferation of one or more other species, which in turn can have cataclysmic effects. Black-footed ferrets used to be quite common, but their extinction in most parts of the country has undoubtedly been caused by the decimation of prairie dogs, the ferret's principal food source.

American mink

Possible Handling Hazards

All of this group have very respectable bites and are inclined to hang on when they have bitten. As with most wild animals, they will prefer to run from a human but are prepared to put up a fight if necessary and are very quick, lithe and agile. The long body is very supple and can bend head to tail so that the teeth can catch you at most points where you might make a grab.

Approach and Capture

The chances of encountering an incapacitated member of this group are fairly remote, but if it should happen, a pair of stout gloves would be distinctly advantageous. Take a quick, firm hold just behind the head with the hand encircling the neck and forequarters. If the animal is lifted from the ground in this manner, there is no way it can bite the handler, and provided the neck is not squeezed, there is no danger to the animal itself. In the case of a weasel a bird-catching net (fig. 1, page 4) might be employed to save having to handle the animal at all, or failing anything else, the "throw a coat over it" routine could be employed.

Transportation

We have never come across or had brought to us an injured member of this group, nor have we ever seen a dead one at the roadside. As a result, the information in this and subsequent parts of the chapter is, to some extent, speculative and is based on experience with tame and captive animals.

Members of the group are not inclined to use their teeth as an aid to escape from a container, although they may, if fit enough to do so, scratch with their front feet in the manner of a dog digging. This is rather ineffectual, however, and a sack should be sufficient to contain the animal for a short journey. For a long distance, a wooden box or a wicker cat basket should fill the bill, so long as you remember that these animals can get through a hole much smaller than might be imagined. Virtually anywhere the head will fit through, the body will, too.

Initial Care

Your patient is unlikely to chew fixtures and fittings and can therefore be kept in any kind of room or shed, but in selecting where it should be kept, we must caution that all of the group possess scent glands from which they can emit an odor, and it is pungent to say the least. In fact, *moderately horrible* are the words that spring to mind to describe the smell, and for anyone brave enough to keep one of the group in a house, the citation must surely read "beyond the call of duty."

Be sure there are no holes through which the animal can escape, and this includes windows. Most of the group are good climbers, so ensure that there is nothing up which they can climb to reach an open window. Apart from indulging in a bit of digging action—which is more likely to be in the water bowl than at a possible point of egress—your patient will probably not be too perturbed by a captive state and should eat readily and heartily.

Food
The pine marten is known to eat a few berries occasionally, as is the fisher, but apart from this, the whole group is carnivorous. Dead day-old chicks, if you can get hold of any (see Chapter 5), will be devoured with alacrity and, if a regular supply can be obtained, could form the principal item of diet. Virtually anything "fish, flesh or fowl" is likely to meet with enthusiastic response, and this does include fish, which will tickle the palate of most. Canned dog food can be used whenever there is nothing else suitable, and a bowl of milk will be lapped up with delight. An occasional raw egg will also go down very well. There is unlikely to be any fastidious sniffing and picking. This is a group which approaches its food with evident lip-smacking enjoyment, leaving nothing on the plate, and any failure to do so is likely to indicate serious internal problems.

Ermine

Force-feeding
Not a very practical proposition.

Symptoms, Diagnosis and Treatment
Members of this group are rarely seen and tend to hide themselves away when sick and injured. They may be found in snares and traps but are usually dead. They are primarily nocturnal, get caught at night and will struggle continuously—to the death—to get free. If they are found alive, the injuries are frequently too severe to heal, and the animal should be taken to a veterinarian to be put to sleep humanely.

General Care

An enclosure such as an aviary, so long as it is covered with very small mesh netting, would be suitable to house one of this group out of doors—but obviously not with birds in residence at the same time. Provide some sort of house where the animal can retire during its sleeping periods and can also shelter itself from bad weather. A wooden box, raised slightly off the ground and covered with a sheet of plastic or roofing felt, would suffice. Bear in mind that most are good climbers, so the enclosure must also have a top covering. Even the overhang recommended for a fox enclosure (see Chapter 13) does not deter one of these agile characters.

Release

These animals can be released virtually anywhere within their normal range and will readily find a niche, although some members of the group must now be considered rare and very localized. It would, of course, be unfair to release any animal where others of its species are not found, so if you are in doubt, the release should only be carried out in consultation with someone who can tell you just where the particular species is to be found if it can't be released in the area it came from (e.g., the Fish and Wildlife Service).

Although all of the group come out during the day from time to time, they should be considered nocturnal animals and released at dusk.

Orphans

It is most unlikely you will meet a suckling infant of one of this group, although an occasional youngster just past the weaning stage is found or carried in by a cat.

Try the youngster first to see if it can lap, in a half-and-half mixture of milk and water. If it can, provide a constant supply in a low dish, as well as some sloppy meat such as canned dog food mixed with a little diluted milk. A pinch of glucose added to the milk will be beneficial.

If the youngster cannot yet lap, feed it as you would baby rabbits (Chapter 10), but always put down a small quantity of solid food, changing it each day, because you will not be sure when your infant will be ready to take it. A shallow dish of milk should also be provided, and bottle feeding should continue for at least a week *after* the infant has started to lap, albeit in reduced quantities, because it will not, at first, be getting enough to sustain it.

The nursery, too, should be as Chapter 10 (page 105).

When the infant is fully furred and active and has been eating and drinking for at least two weeks, it can be transferred outside, but do provide warm bedding in the sleeping box—hay, for instance. Retain the animal in the enclosure until the autumn or possibly even until the following spring to give it a good start, although the animal may well be too dependent by that time for a release to a completely wild existence. The odd one or two we have reared have been past the bottle stage when they came in. They were not handled unduly and retained an air of independence. Incidentally, these have only been weasels.

Weasel

In general, if the animal can be released directly from the enclosure in which it has been living, we would recommend giving it a try, while continuing to provide food in the enclosure to which it has free access.

13

Wolves, Foxes and Coyotes

We hear some very strange identifications from time to time. For instance, "a duck with a long neck and long legs" turns out to be a bittern, or a red deer hind is described as "a thin brown donkey." In the case of the fox there should be no such confusion. Although many people have never seen a fox "in the flesh," it is extremely unlikely that anyone would fail to recognize the adult animal.

Small kits, however, bear little resemblance to their parents. They have gray coats instead of the adult red, rather flat faces and stringy little tails, which give no hint of the magnificent brushes they will become. On one occasion we almost came to blows with a man who brought in a small dead animal for us to identify. He had already informed press and television—presumably with visions of triumphant appearances as the finder of some hitherto-unknown species—and was most upset when we told him that his "find" was a fox kit. He snatched back the little body, declaring that we didn't know what we were talking about, and stormed from the premises. We subsequently learned that he had called on the local museum curator, several local wildlife groups and a zoo in an endeavor to obtain a more exotic identification.

The saying "Give a dog a bad name" could have been devised especially for this group, which is blamed for just about everything short of bank robbery, even though much of the evidence doesn't stand up to close scrutiny. It is often claimed, for instance, that foxes kill domestic cats. We have never encountered a single authenticated case of this having happened. On the contrary, what we *have* seen is a film of a red fox and a cat passing one another, albeit warily, along a path. The fox isn't noted for its bravery, and it is extremely unlikely it would attack a cat, which would make a formidable adversary. There are many easier pickings, and if the fox is not brave, it is undoubtedly resourceful and adaptable.

Another piece of "foxlore" of doubtful authenticity is that of a fox "charming" its prey. The fox is alleged to roll around, chase its tail and generally act the fool, thereby engaging the curiosity of any mentally deficient rabbits in the vicinity. The fox contrives to gradually move closer to the mesmerized rabbits until close enough to pounce on the nearest, thereby securing a tasty meal with the minimum of effort.

Accusations abound of attacks on lambs, and occasionally the stomach contents of dead foxes and coyotes certainly have revealed the presence of wool. Eyewitness accounts of actual attacks, however, are rare. So, while not entirely ruling out the possibility of such an attack on occasion, we consider it much more likely that the lambs are usually dead or dying and have been abandoned by the ewe before the fox appears on the scene.

There is no doubt that earlier in the century coyotes did do considerable damage among domestic livestock, but it wasn't until the government hired trappers that farmers began to realize coyotes also had a beneficial effect in keeping the rodent population under control. It also became clear that coyotes did, in fact, usually carry off only the injured, sick and weaker stock. So, in 1953, in Colorado, a group of farmers formed an association which prohibited the use of poisoned bait within a 250,000-acre area. It was dramatically successful, for by doing this, the farmers gained far more than they lost.

Coyote

Careful research by the Fish and Wildlife Service reveals the diet of coyotes to comprise 33 percent hares and rabbits, 25 percent carrion, 18 percent rodents, 10.5 percent of miscellaneous items and only 13.5 percent of sheep and goats.

A trick which coyotes have learned and is most amusing is to "employ" a badger. What happens is that when a badger is digging for rodents, a coyote will wait by one of the burrow escape holes for any of the residents trying to escape the badger's attentions and will pounce on any emerging!

It cannot be denied that a fox will wreak havoc in a chicken house. Many would (and do) say this is pure blood lust, though a more plausible explanation would surely be instinctive opportunism, directing the animal to provide for more than its immediate needs when the chance is offered. The fox regularly hides rodents, for instance, that it doesn't immediately need to eat, to dig up later when times are lean. We ourselves go off to a supermarket and buy up enough food to last a week or more and consider this perfectly rational behavior. What's so different about the fox attempting to do the same?

Wolves are much feared, but with little cause. For one thing, attacks on humans are more in legend than in fact. There have been very few authenticated cases. For another thing, you are unlikely to encounter a wolf anyway. Since the prospects of encountering a wolf casualty are virtually nil and a coyote casualty quite remote, we will focus the remainder of the chapter on foxes, although both wolves and coyotes *can* be maintained in captivity and most of the ensuing information *could* apply.

Although there is nothing wrong with its dental equipment, a fox is unlikely to offer the direct jaw-clamping bite a dog might inflict. There will be no attempt to bite at all until a hand is almost touching, and even then it will be only a glancing snap, often accompanied by a terrified yelp as it attempts to escape.

A handling hazard which must never be overlooked is rabies. Skunks are the commonest carriers in the United States (see Chapter 16), but all of this group are also potential transmitters.

Approach, Capture and Transportation

It is reasonable to assume that there is something wrong with any fox that fails to move off quickly. As with most wildlife casualties, the fox will try to reach hiding, even if it is only partially mobile, and this can help you gather up a casualty. A good-sized wooden box will make a suitable traveling container. If the animal can move at all and the box is placed in his line of retreat with the opening toward him and a sack or cloth over most of the opening, it may well appear to be a welcome haven. The fox can be encouraged to go in the right direction with the aid of one or two large pieces of flat board in the manner of herding pigs, preventing escape to the side.

If it is necessary to lift the animal, the use of a dog

grasper (fig. 13) is recommended since this removes all possibility of a bite. If such an implement or the materials to make one are not available, one hand (preferably gloved) should be moved slowly, but in full view, toward the animal's nose. When it makes a snap, this hand is withdrawn and the other hand takes a very firm grasp of the scruff. Normally once a fox feels itself firmly held in this manner, it will make no further attempt to struggle. Maintaining the grasp on the scruff, the free hand can be employed to lift the casualty into the container. This operation is not as difficult as it sounds. The fox is not a very strong animal, and this, coupled with its tendency to lie dormant when held, means that a grip on its scruff is easier to maintain than that on a terrier dog. The weaker hand—the left hand of a right-handed person—should be the "bait," and a better grip can be achieved if the gripping hand is bare.

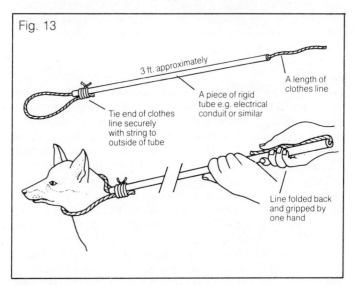

Fig. 13

3 ft. approximately

A length of clothes line

A piece of rigid tube e.g. electrical conduit or similar

Tie end of clothes line securely with string to outside of tube

Line folded back and gripped by one hand

Initial Care
Wherever the fox is to be accommodated, it is a sound idea to allow it to keep the traveling container as a substitute den. The less changing, the better, and the container will already feel comforting and familiar by the time the destination is reached, no matter how short the journey. A feeling of security is all-important to the animal's peace of mind.

A wild fox does *not* make the ideal houseguest. If not as bad as those in the previous chapter, the smell it can emit is still quite strong in a confined space. A garage, outhouse or garden shed would be best to accommodate the patient for a short period, and a thick covering of sawdust is recommended for the floor (even if this is changed regularly, it will take a long time to get rid of the smell when your guest has departed!). In the early stages of treatment the garage or shed will be adequate for an injured fox, provided that everyone in the neighborhood isn't invited to come and have a look. However, in the convalescent stages a wooden shed may not do since some foxes will try to chew their way out. This is by no means standard practice. We have had many foxes that have made no such attempt, even when confined for lengthy periods. But there is no way of knowing in advance whether or not your particular fox will be a chewer, so keep a careful watch. A few slivers of wood gnawed from a doorpost is sufficient warning that a change to chewproof accommodation is needed.

Food

Feeding is quite easy, for the average fox will take readily to canned dog or cat food and, indeed, will eat most kitchen scraps. As a regular diet, while in captivity, canned dog food mixed with dog biscuit will be perfectly satisfactory, and the quantity should be the same as that recommended on the can for a dog of comparable size to the fox. One feeding per day is sufficient for an adult, and if the food fails to disappear, the fox's mouth and jaw should be examined for injury because most foxes could be described as "chowhounds" even in the most adverse circumstances.

A bowl of clean water should be available at all times and inspected frequently, for many foxes, for reasons best known to them, urinate in their water bowls. This can be somewhat trying when you've just washed the bowl and provided nice clean water, particularly if you've had to carry it some distance. All foxes don't do it, and you might be lucky enough to have one with more decorum.

If there should be any temporary feeding problem but the animal can still lap, milk and any kind of baby cereal or even a good thick meat soup will be most acceptable.

Force-feeding foxes is inadvisable.

Symptoms, Diagnosis and Treatment

A fox that is sick or injured will invariably try to return to its den or go into hiding to "lick its wounds." It is likely, therefore, that foxes that are come across are the worst cases, needing much treatment, care and attention. If they are too badly injured or diseased, it may be kinder to put them to sleep to cut short their suffering.

The commonest causes of disability are road accidents, capture in snares or traps, poisoning and disease.

Injuries. Road accidents are not uncommon, for though the fox is intelligent and fast on its feet, and it has discovered that the car will not usually chase it through hedges and across fields—or if it does, it is not as persistent in pursuit as the horse and hound—the animal often misjudges the speed. The majority of accident injuries are to the rear end of the animal—cuts and bruises and fractures of limbs, pelvis and spine. Of course, some foxes are struck on the body and head and neck region. In addition to bruising and laceration, many suffer internal injuries, perhaps hemorrhage and shock. From a recent study of more than 300 foxes killed in London in various ways, 91 had healed fractures, 24 had broken ribs, 42 had fractures of the spine and tail, 16 involved the pelvis, 29 the hindlimb, and 23 the forelimb. Altogether 41 percent involved the forequarters and 59 percent the hindquarters.

Broken legs can be diagnosed by their awkward appearance. The limb bends where there is no joint, and often a grating noise can be heard when it is moved. There is often damage to the skin, which may be broken and bleeding. If major limb bones are fractured, the animal is unable to use the limb and will drag it. In the forelimb this can be confused with paralysis caused by damage to the radial nerve. When minor limb bones are affected, the animal can move the limb but is obviously in pain and will not usually walk on it. It limps visibly by throwing its head up when the affected limb touches the ground and comes down heavily on the normal limb.

Fractures of the pelvis cause various symptoms, depending on the site of the break. In some cases, apart from pain, little can be observed. In other cases the animal may have difficulty in walking and may sway awkwardly from side to side.

Fractures of the spine usually cause a great deal of pain, and if the spinal cord (the nerve trunk running down the spine) is nipped or damaged, there could be loss of feeling below or behind the injury.

Internal injuries, such as damage to the liver, are difficult to diagnose. The mucous membranes of the eye and mouth become pale or bluish if there is internal bleeding. But this is also a symptom of shock.

Capture in snares and traps is common. Snares often catch the fox around the neck, or neck and one foreleg, causing strangulation and severe damage to skin and tissues. The poor animal, finding itself caught, pulls and tugs to escape. The snare tightens, and the animal may lose consciousness and collapse. The snare may then go slack, and the creature regains consciousness to begin its struggles again. If the fox is caught by its leg, it usually struggles till the wire cuts deeply into or through the limb.

Traps cause as much damage. Not only do they inflict severe lacerations, but the trapped animal sometimes chews off its foot in its effort to escape. Often the skin is stripped off and the bones are exposed.

Diseases and Poisoning. The symptoms of poisoning depend on the types of poison used. Strychnine causes periodic simultaneous contractions of all the muscles, producing cramplike pain. The exterior muscles are more powerful so the animal's limbs are extended, the back bent concavely with the head thrown back and the facial muscles pulled tight. After a few seconds the muscles relax. Any small stimulus will cause contraction again. Gradually the contraction periods get longer and the interval of relaxation less until the animal dies of asphyxia.

The other common type of poisoning is by pesticides such as malathion or parathion, which belong to a group called organophosphorus compounds. These substances act on insects and animals by interfering with the action of an enzyme in the nervous system; this causes a state of chaos. The symptoms are depression, muscular weakness, diarrhea and eventually prostration. Symptoms appear within twenty-four hours of exposure and last for several days. Smaller doses cause chronic poisoning, muscular twitching, loss of weight and diarrhea that may persist for weeks.

Warfarin poisoning sometimes occurs because foxes occasionally eat meal in which the poison is laid, usually for rats. It interferes with the clotting mechanism of the blood and produces symptoms of weakness, bloody diarrhea and hemorrhage throughout the body muscles, particularly over bony prominences, and in the joints, causing lameness.

A poison called compound 1080, which has been used in the past for coyote control and was banned in 1972, could be licensed again if some ranchers have their way, for they say that coyotes are again becoming a major problem. Government trappers are available on request, however, and in 1981 they killed 57,138, using mainly M-44s, which are small booby traps loaded with cyanide and planted in the ground. Conservationists are worried that a reintroduction of compound 1080 will lead to the death of a lot of other wildlife, too. This would be less likely if the poison were used in bags attached to collars around the necks of sheep. In this way, only coyotes involved in killing would die. However, there may be a great temptation to bait carcasses.

Red fox

Distemper is a virus disease affecting all doglike species as well as a variety of other wild carnivores. The animal develops a fever, with a discharge from the eyes and nose, and usually diarrhea. The mortality rate is high, from 20 to 90 percent in captive species. What happens in the wild is unknown. Treatment is unlikely to prove successful in returning the animal to a state where it can be released.

The most common disease in foxes is mange—a skin infection caused by a minute spiderlike creature called *Sarcoptes*. It is transmitted by contact and gradually spreads over the animal's body, causing loss of hair and a thickening of the skin.

Treatment of the more serious accidents, trap and snare injuries, and of poisoning and diseases should be left to a veterinarian. First aid can be given, however— wounds bandaged; hemorrhage stopped by placing a pad of gauze on the bleeding point and binding it tight enough to occlude the vessel; shock treated by protecting the animal from cold and keeping it quiet. Though veterinary treatment is usually necessary, it is only part of the story. Good nursing and aftercare are essential to success. It is interesting that the fox is much less persistent than the domestic dog in chewing and worrying at the bandage or plaster. Very often the fox will completely ignore it.

The treatment the veterinarian will use for fractures varies with the bone that is broken and the type of fracture. In some cases it may be sufficient to bandage the area, others may require a plaster cast, while some can be pinned with metal rods or plates. The vet will probably suture nearly all wounds and may give the animal a shot of a long-acting antibiotic. If a paw is badly injured, part of it may be amputated. But because the fox will eventually be released, nothing that will seriously reduce its future ability to capture his food is usually done.

Strychnine poisoning can often be successfully treated by a vet, for the poison does not persist indefinitely in the animal's body. The usual treatment is to keep the animal relaxed under anesthesia (usually barbiturate) until the poison has been dealt with by the animal's metabolic processes.

Pesticide persists for a long time and interferes with the animal's automatic function, and the prognosis is less hopeful.

Mange can be treated with one of the special insecticide dressings, provided the disease does not cover too much of the animal's body, for the dressing is poisonous. It must be applied at regular intervals, over five to seven days, because one treatment is not enough.

General Care

If the fox needs to be kept for a prolonged period, an outdoor pen is desirable. This should be constructed of material stronger than ordinary wire netting—A semirigid wire mesh of at least 16 gauge or chain link with a mesh size about 2 × 2 inches is most satisfactory. But it must be remembered that a fox can (and will) both dig and climb. It will scale a wire mesh fence with consummate ease but will be completely baffled by an overhang of about eighteen inches (fig. 14). To counter any digging, similar wire mesh must be placed on the ground covering about three feet all around the inside of the perimeter and firmly fixed to the bottom of the fence. It is *not* necessary to cover the whole ground area of the pen since the fox will invariably try to dig at the base of the fence. We have not yet encountered one resourceful enough to work out that in order to get under the fence, digging operations must commence three feet in from the base.

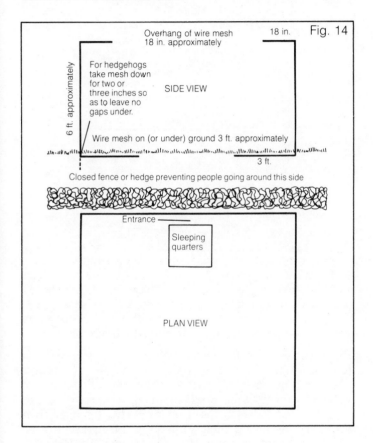

A small house of some kind must be provided as a den, just as in the indoor accommodation. The animal will not be unduly perturbed at the approach of people so long as it can rapidly get completely out of sight. For this reason, the entrance to the house must be set in such a way that anyone approaching cannot see into it and cannot reach that side of the pen (fig. 15). If the original traveling box is still serviceable, it can be made reasonably weatherproof with the addition of a sheet of plastic over the top and sides, and it should be used in preference to a new residence. To misquote an old saying, "Familiarity breeds content."

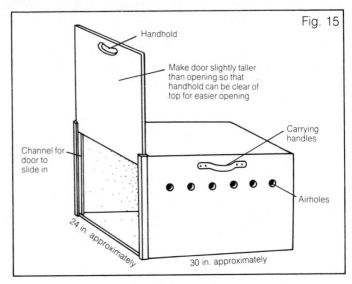

Fig. 15

Handhold

Make door slightly taller than opening so that handhold can be clear of top for easier opening

Carrying handles

Channel for door to slide in

Airholes

24 in. approximately

30 in. approximately

There is no easy way to keep an outside pen clean and odor-free unless it is concrete-based and can be hosed regularly. A foul-smelling pen may quickly undermine the sympathy and tolerance of neighbors, so place the pen as far away as possible from their houses.

Release

Release of an adult casualty must be at the earliest possible moment consistent with a reasonable chance of survival. There is an understandable tendency among wildlife first-aiders to hold on to patients longer than necessary, doubting their ability to cope again with the rough-and-tumble life in the wild. If you are in doubt, it is probably time for the animal to go take its chances. There is little likelihood of a fox caught as an adult becoming imprinted (see "Orphans"), but prolonged captivity may well dull the sharp edge of awareness necessary to survive in the wild.

If release can be effected on the animal's home ground, this in itself will contribute to its chance of survival, but the fox is very adaptable and will quickly find a niche in almost any situation, provided it is released within the normal range for the particular species concerned.

Orphans

If a normally wild animal is not afraid of people, someone will undoubtedly kill it unless it is living in a sheltered environment, a sad reflection on the human race. Fox kits are quite easy to raise but imprinting (losing the fear of and becoming dependent on humans) is a major problem, particularly when there is only one kit to be reared.

Finding a solitary infant of a species that normally produces more than one (a fox litter averages four) gives grounds for suspicion that there may be something wrong which has caused the parent to reject and abandon this particular offspring, although there may be nothing readily apparent. We had a fox kit brought to us on one occasion with its eyes only just opening, meaning that it was no more than two weeks old (the eyes open for the first time at about ten days). We could find nothing wrong and set about rearing the kit. About three weeks later we realized it was mentally deficient. It would seem the mother had detected something amiss much earlier than we did.

Before you undertake the raising of fox kits, the implications should be fully appreciated, not least of which is the length of time they will have to be kept. In the wild, if they have not been dug out earlier, fox kits will emerge from their den at about the beginning of May, when they are about four weeks old. It is at this time of year that most stray kits are picked up. They would part from the mother, in the normal course of events, during late August or early September, and we consider that this is when those reared in captivity should be released—so a stay of some four months is the minimum.

The prospect of a fox kit imprinted on humans returning successfully to the wild is very remote. Having no fear of humans will prove a fatal affliction even if the animal is able to fend for itself. For this reason, we do not recommend that anyone should attempt to rear a single fox kit unless he or she intends to keep the animal as a pet.

It is possible to keep a fox as a pet, but we do not recommend this either. In our experience the experiment rarely succeeds. A fox does not take at all kindly to being moved from one home to another (during holidays, etc.), and more often than not the animal eventually has to be destroyed. Our advice, if you find yourself in possession of a single kit, is to try to find someone else in similar circumstances, possibly via the local state rehabilitation center (consult the Fish and Wildlife Service) or even the local news media, and to raise the kits together. They needn't be from the same family; we regularly rear groups of up to a dozen all from different families and from different parts of the country. Ideally more than one person should be involved in the rearing, as will be explained.

Fox kit

If the kits are too young to feed themselves, if they have been dug out, we recommend feeding them Borden's Esbilac, obtainable from most pet stores. Follow the instructions for quantities and frequency of feeding for puppies which are on the side of every can. A plastic syringe without the needle is useful for administering it. Always leave a dish of Esbilac on the floor as well since the kits will start helping themselves much sooner than you would think from their size. As soon as they are able to lap, provide a dish of solid food also. Canned dog food mixed with puppy meal will serve quite satisfactorily.

It must be remembered that if the kits are from different litters, they will not necessarily be of the same age, so take care that they *all* can feed themselves before the bottle/syringe feeding is finished.

If possible, when weaning has been completed, the person who has been doing the bottle feeding of the kits, and therefore the handling, should drop out of the scene and never go near them again. This is because there will have been a measure of imprinting caused by the handling and bottle feeding but, at this stage, one hopes, only on that one person. The person taking over after weaning must *never* handle the kits and indeed must frighten them off should they venture near.

Kits should be provided with a dark box for a den to which they can run and hide. The box need not be very large. They seem to prefer it snug so that they can pack in like sardines. We have found a box approximately 30 × 24 × 24 inches is sufficient for up to five kits, even when they are quite well grown. The box should be portable with some means of closing the entrance when the kits are inside and with adequate ventilation when the box is closed. The reason will become apparent later.

After weaning, one good meal a day is all that is necessary, and the more squabbling and fighting over it, the better. We use mainly dead day-old chicks from a local hatchery and even dead-in-shell chicks, which we feed complete with shell. The idea, held by some, that this will give the kits a taste for poultry is erroneous. Foxes have a taste for vitually anything edible, and a steady diet of chicks does not preclude their falling upon anything else which might come within reach. Nor will it give them a preference for chicks over other food; they will eat anything that requires the minimum of effort.

Fresh water should always be available, although foxes do not appear to drink a great deal. The earlier remarks about the unsavory habits of some adult foxes with their water bowls also apply to kits, with the added refinement that some kits are apt to defecate in them, too, just for good measure!

By the time of release, indeed from the time of the second person's taking over, the kits should be ready and willing to bite the hand that feeds them and should flee to the safety of their den at the approach of any human. They should also have the strongest possible objection to being handled or molested in any way.

There are two ways in which release can be effected, neither of which involves any handling. The first is simply to open the door of the pen, allowing the kits to make their own way into the world beyond. Continue putting food into the pen so that they can return for a meal should they wish to do so. Although this is undoubtedly the best way to release them, in most cases it simply isn't practicable for one reason or another.

The second way is to shut the kits in their box when they run in to hide (hence the door) and to transport them to the point of release. This should be as far away as possible from human habitation and preferably in a piece of rough woodland. The permission of the landowner must be given first, of course. The box should if possible be left at the release point, and the release effected by just opening the door. The box will afford the kits an orientation point, and if food can be left in the vicinity for several days, so much the better. There will be no way of knowing whether or not it is the kits that are eating the food, unless someone can spare the time to keep watch, but it *may* just help them get started on their independent lives.

The kits will not remain where they are released and will quickly have to face all the hazards which are the price of a free-living existence. At least you'll know you've done the best you can; the rest is up to them. We have reared and released many kits in the manner described and, from observations made, believe it to be a successful formula.

14

Otters and Other Aquatics

Books such as *Tarka the Otter* and *Ring of Bright Water* have done much to carve out a place in the affections of most people for the lively otter. It is a playful and altogether delightful little animal, but few people have ever seen one, and even fewer have actually seen one in its wild state.

In North America there are two species of otter, both of which have been hunted, poisoned and polluted to the verge of extinction. Even now, in this more conservation-conscious era, both have only a tenuous hold on existence. A comparatively minor oil spill, for instance, could easily destroy the entire sea otter population off the coast of California, yet, ironically, here is an animal absolutely brimming over with *joi de vivre*, spending much of its time in playful pursuits. The river otter will construct a slide for the sole purpose of having good wholesome fun, sliding into the water, then scampering out to do it again and again, while its sea relative will spontaneously play, alone or with others of its kind or even with seals or sea lions.

Sea otters are also among the exclusive few animals in the world to use tools. In the case of the sea otter, this takes the form of diving for a shellfish and at the same time bringing up a small rock, which is then placed on the otter's chest. While the animal floats on its back, it hammers the shellfish on the rock vigorously in order to break the shell—a most amusing process to watch.

Others we are including in this chapter are the muskrat, two of which are native to the United States, the nutria and the beaver. In appearance, the otters resemble overgrown weasels (and indeed belong to the same family), while the rest of the group resemble woodchucks (apart from the tails, which are much more adapted to an aquatic way of life). It is often said, by the way, that much of the wealth of the United States owes its foundation to the profits from beaver trapping in the last century and early part of this one.

Apart from being hunted, these shy, elusive and sensitive creatures haven't taken kindly to the recent great increase in the use of waterways for many and diverse leisure pursuits. Pesticides draining from fields into streams, and a thousand and one other kinds of pollution flowing indiscriminately into rivers, do not help provide a viable environment. Nor does the draining of marshlands—now being done on a grand scale—which is a disaster for many other wild creatures besides the otter.

In the past twenty or so years vast strides have been made in the cleaning up of waterways and the monitoring of what goes into them. Unfortunately this very cleanup, which should, on the face of it, provide an altogether happier outlook for the otter, has instead generated a vast increase in human use of waterways. These animals just can't win, can they?

Possible Handling Hazards
It would be more correct to head this section "Probable handling hazards." Any attempt to handle an adult otter in possession of all its faculties, even with the use of thick gloves, would be most foolhardy and would almost certainly result in one or more very severe bites, with the loss of one or more fingers a distinct risk (and the subsequent loss of a hand not beyond the bounds of possibility). The otter's body is very supple as well as very strong, and the animal is able to reach virtually any part of its anatomy with its formidable teeth, so there is no place it can be grabbed with impunity. The other group members, too, have formidable biting equipment, which should be treated with the greatest respect. Teeth which can fell a four-inch diameter tree in about three minutes flat (as a beaver's can) are most certainly not to be underestimated!

Approach and Capture
If the animal is mobile, the chances of approach are minimal unless the animal has suffered a moderate to severe injury. If an otter in particular *should* be found, every effort should be made to save it and return it to the wild, where every individual animal is of the utmost importance.

Members of this group can be lifted with a dog grasper

(see Chapter 13) but not around the neck. The noose must go over both neck and forequarters (front legs); otherwise it is likely to slip off when you attempt to lift it. When the animal is in the traveling container, the noose can easily be released by allowing the line to slide right through the handle (from the handle end). It can be rethreaded later.

An alternate method is to tangle the animal up in a piece of heavy netting of any sort, taking care to keep the hands well clear. This will allow a veterinarian to administer an anesthetic through the netting without much danger of being bitten, and the animal can then be untangled for an inspection either prior to or after the journey.

River otter

If no dog grasper or netting is available, a tablecloth or sheet might be eased under an immobile animal with two people holding the edges taut and using a sort of sawing action. You can then lift the cloth by the corners and deposit both the cloth and the patient in the traveling container.

Transportation

A wood or metal container is preferable. Failing that, a sack will probably suffice for the journey. This group is not inclined to make much of a fuss when in a container, and an injured one will welcome the seclusion.

Initial Care

An otter will be unlikely to chew at the woodwork or demolish the fixtures and fittings, although it may attack any exposed electric wires (which should be well out of reach). If a suitable bolt hole, such as a wooden chest placed on its side with the open end facing a wall and about nine inches (twenty-two centimeters) away from it, is provided, and the open end partly covered with a sack or cloth, the otter will doubtless be grateful for this and will be happy to keep out of sight. With these provisos, any room can be used as a temporary residence (although obviously a bit of a mess will be made on the floor, so don't endanger your best Persian carpet!).

Left to its own devices, a beaver might well demolish anything made of wood, so bear this well in mind when selecting a place to keep one; otherwise you might find a new dining table reduced to firewood!

Food

The otter is quite a good eater, the river otter consuming about twenty pounds of food per week in the wild. Items on the menu include fish—principally what are called trash fish (contrary to what many anglers think)—frogs, newts, the odd duckling, rabbits and small rodents. When otters "summer" at the seaside, crabs and sundry other creatures found in the shallows are high on the list of favorite delicacies, but taking precedence over all others are eels. The average otter will sell its soul for an eel, so for the otter captivity, chopped or whole eels are an obvious appetite tempter. Other items which can be offered are minced raw beef, whitefish and dead day-old chicks. Water should, of course, also be provided.

A sea otter's diet consists of various shellfish, sea urchins, crabs, etc., but you are *very* unlikely to be called upon to feed a sea otter. If the "very unlikely" should happen (as it is apt to do when somebody has told you it won't), we would recommend seeking out a specializing establishment and handing it over immediately (consult the Fish and Wildlife Service).

The other group members are principally vegetarian. Offer a selection of fruit and vegetables, greens in particular, and, for a beaver, a steady supply of tree branches and twigs. If you'll pardon the pun, poplar seems the most popular, but most others will be accepted.

Incidentally, it is normal for the nutria to eat some of its own feces in the same way that hares and rabbits do.

Symptoms, Diagnosis and Treatment

Though extremely playful, otters do occasionally bite each other, and probably because the animal is continually in water, wounds tend to become infected. When otters are in captivity, wounds should be kept clean and antibiotics administered daily.

An abscess may sometimes develop inside the mouth. If it is very large, the animal should be anesthetized, the abscess opened and drained, and a dosage of antibiotic given until it has healed. Smaller abscesses may be treated with antibiotic alone.

A mouth abscess is dangerous because should it burst in the mouth, there is a danger of the otter's inhaling the pus and contracting pneumonia. This disease is not uncommon in otters, probably because they are constantly in water. Anything that damages the coat and allows water to penetrate may lead to pneumonia. The animal stops eating, its coat becomes disheveled and unkempt and the eyes become dull and watery. Later there may be a discharge from the nose.

These symptoms also occur, however, with tularemia and with leptospirosis, a disease of the kidneys and liver. These affect the other members of the group, and they can also affect humans.

A fatal disease of muskrats with a rather long-winded name is epizootic chlamydiosis. It is caused by a small organism. Like many infectious diseases, its spread is probably encouraged by high density of population—think what trouble Western society would be in were it not for sewage disposal and other sanitary measures!

Beaver

General Care

When convalescent, an otter should have access to a pool as well as to a large outdoor paddock. It is most unlikely, however, short of a considerable financial outlay, that the average person could provide suitable temporary accommodation at this stage in the proceedings. We therefore recommend that the animal be passed on, as soon as possible, to some place fully equipped and experienced to offer it the optimum possible chance of survival. Holding on to *any* animal that might have better prospects elsewhere can be construed only as self-indulgence.

Release

River otters range over quite long distances, so if one is found injured, it is extremely difficult to judge just where it was coming from or going to. If you find one during a hot summer when streams are getting a bit low, it was probably on its way to the seaside. As with other species with sparse populations, as much advice as possible should be sought before effecting a release. The otters are fairly widespread, within their normal ranges.

Orphans

Apart from the beaver, young of this group seem to be born at any time during the year, so there is no set·time when you may find orphans. The chances of coming across a youngster are remote, but it is not unknown. The usual cause in such a case is the parent being hit by a car and killed, leaving the youngster or youngsters wandering vaguely about, not knowing what to do without mom to show them. Any picked up at this stage will be in the region of ten weeks old and quite able to survive happily on a solid diet with no necessity to be bottle-fed, although a drop of Esbilac or something similar (see Appendix C) in a dish may well meet with approval.

The chances of finding youngsters that need bottle feeding are even more remote and would depend on some calamitous circumstance affecting the actual nursery. Should this occur, very young infants are unlikely to survive long enough on their own to come to the notice of a possible benefactor.

For their first few weeks the infants are possibly slightly less robust than badger cubs of the same age, but they can be treated in the same way for initial care and feeding. Badgers belong to the same family as otters, although they don't look much like the other members.

Hand-reared otter cubs are apt to become very tame. Tameness does not bode well for their prospects in the wild, so as with adults, it is imperative that any youngsters found should be handed on as quickly as possible to experts. They can then be given every opportunity for a possible self-sufficient existence or, failing that, at least a reasonable quality of life.

One other animal that should perhaps be mentioned in this chapter is the mountain beaver. We say "perhaps" because it isn't really a beaver at all and is not what you would call aquatic except that it likes a lot of moisture in its burrows and sometimes will divert a stream into its burrow system.

You are even less likely to come across one of these than the other group members since it is confined to the Far West of the Far West and is an extremely shy animal.

The porcupine has similar tastes in food to the beaver and could well be included here. Even if you'd never seen even a picture of one, you would easily recognize it by the description alone, its being the only character in the United States wearing a coat resembling a whole armory of spears!

There are a couple of points to bear in mind, if you

are ever called upon to deal with one of these prickly individuals, one about handling and one about general care and housing.

The idea that a porcupine can actually shoot its spines at an adversary is untrue, but what it can and will do is lash out with its tail, and if any of the spines should stick in said adversary, the porcupine can then release them, there being a sort of quick release mechanism at the porcupine's end.

There are tiny barbs at the "business" end of each spine which swell up to retain the spine and make it difficult to remove, should the adversary be another animal. If you should be unfortunate enough to be so caught, cut a piece off the other end of the spine. They are hollow, and cutting them will release pressure, allowing the spine to be more easily withdrawn.

Porcupines have a phenomenal craving for salt, and they eat, or attempt to eat, anything you have handled. If housed in a garden shed, your client will very probably demolish the handles of all your tools as well as eat your gardening gloves!

15

Marine Mammals

Around the coasts of North America live many marine mammals, including three species of eared seal or sea lion, five haired seals, a walrus, many species of whales and dolphins and the manatee.

The seals live and breed on various parts of the coast, on islands or in secluded coves. Some species live on ice floes in the sea. Whales, dolphins and manatees, although they are air-breathing mammals, never come ashore in normal circumstances.

All of the sea lions, two of the haired seals and perhaps the walrus may be seen along the coast of the United States. They are quite distinctive from any purely land-based mammal in general appearance, the principal difference, of course, being that they have no feet. This makes them very ungainly on land, although they can move faster than might be imagined. Few people would fail to recognize a seal or a sea lion, but not many could distinguish between the two. Looking closely, you will see the small ears of the sea lions. Sea lions also have generally more slender bodies and longer necks than seals.

Most people also have a fair idea of what a dolphin and a whale look like, having seen them in captivity or on television in one of the many films which deal with the plight of these highly intelligent creatures, abused and persecuted almost beyond belief. The United States enjoys a great variety of these wonderful animals in the coastal seas, and other species pass by on their migration over hundreds of miles.

Porpoises and dolphins, also members of the whale family, are more often seen, and great numbers are killed by tuna fishermen, who lay out huge nets around tuna shoals, also imprisoning the dolphins (which have guided the fishermen there in the first place). The bridled dolphin has probably suffered most in this way with something between 20,000 and 40,000 being killed each year (about half by U.S. fishermen), but other species are also affected, and up to the 1960s around half a million dolphins were being killed each year. In 1972 the Marine Mammal Protection Act helped reduce the carnage.

You may ask why such intelligent animals allow themselves to be caught and killed in this way. Are they *really* as intelligent as people say they are? Perhaps one recorded incident will suffice to convince you that in some ways at least, they are indeed very intelligent. It is recorded in a wonderful book on whales by Lyall Watson, *Guide to Whales of the World*. A human observer was looking through the glass side of a dolphin tank, and a young dolphin was looking out at him. The man was smoking at the time and blew smoke toward the animal. The young dolphin immediately sought its mother and returned with a mouthful of milk. When the observer was at the window again, it blew the milk toward him, producing the same effect in the water as the smoke had done in air!

The manatee is a species apart. Although it looks roughly similar to a seal, it is a herbivorous mammal, more closely related to land-based herbivorous mammals. It is found only in the southeastern Atlantic coastal waters, around to the Gulf of Mexico, with its main "beat" around Florida. Because the manatee is very slow-moving and not too aware, a great deal of damage to the species has been caused by the propellers of the greatly increased boating community of the postwar years. This, coupled with general disturbance, has put the manatee on the danger list, and efforts are now being made to minimize the dangers. Incidentally, this species is thought to be the original "mermaid," although it doesn't look much like the mermaid in the imagination of the average seaman!

Whales and dolphins become stranded from time to time, sometimes singly but often in groups. The most common species involved are the common dolphin, the bottlenose dolphin and the pilot whale, although other larger species are sometimes involved. Not all the animals are giants—the common is only about five feet in length, and the pilot whale can reach a length of twenty-eight feet, but this is still modest by whale standards.

There is no certainty as to the reason or reasons why whales and dolphins become stranded. One possibility is that the animals may be seeking safety from drowning. Because they are air-breathing mammals, this can, of course, happen. Unlike the respiration of land mammals, their breathing is not automatic but under conscious control, and if an animal should feel itself losing consciousness, it may seek shallow water in order to keep its blowhole above the surface. In some parts of the world beached whales have been found to have parasitic worms in the inner ears which may have caused loss of balance and probably were extremely painful. Indeed, many infected animals have serious self-inflicted injuries of the skin above the ear area, apparently caused by rubbing against jagged rocks. The bodies of some other beached whales have poisonous amounts of mercury *in their bodies* which may have caused mental derangement. Some whales, apparently fit and healthy, are thought to have been following a school of fish inshore and inadvertently became stranded when the tide receded. Mass strandings sometimes occur, and a possible cause is that one animal becomes sick and the others rally around to go to its aid.

Possible Handling Hazards

There is little danger from a stranded whale or dolphin. It is completely helpless when well clear of the water, and although all of those mentioned possess quite formidable teeth, only the most idiotic of persons is likely to suffer any damage from them. Seals, on the other hand, also have quite respectable dental equipment which they are not averse to using. Even the youngest of them will defend itself vigorously against any attempt at handling, and very severe, possibly crippling bites can result. There is a further danger from a seal bite in that it may result in a pathogenic infection requiring antibiotic treatment.

Approach and Capture

Approaching a stranded whale or dolphin is easy since the animal is unable to move and the question of "capture" does not arise.

A seal should be approached from the rear. If it is necessary to catch it, take hold only of the hind flippers. Nowhere else is really safe, even with a tiny pup. And handling a sea lion can be even more hazardous. The first sea lion we ever had to examine and treat had several nasty wounds and either a fever or pneumonia causing an accelerated respiratory rate. We surveyed her dubiously, and she eyed us with grave suspicion; then she opened her mouth and hissed as though to say, "Just keep your distance if you know what's good for you." Nobody was wildly enthusiastic, and something had to be done, but where do you get hold of an animal that is perfectly streamlined with nothing to get hold *of*? We got a door and, holding it horizontally, pressed her into a confined area. Then it was Bill's turn. He wanted to examine her chest but had to abandon the idea when he very nearly had an ear bitten off. We squeezed her tighter and held a crosspiece behind her neck while Bill jabbed her with a large dose of antibiotic in what he thought was a safe place. He just managed it before she turned completely around in that small space and her teeth closed, with an audible snap, a few inches from his hand.

Transportation

This issue is unlikely to arise in the case of whales and dolphins, but if it does, it is undoubtedly a matter for experts (see following section). It is a comparatively easy task to maneuver a small seal pup into a suitable container, which need be only a shallow box large enough to contain it comfortably, with no top necessary since seals aren't very good at jumping! For an adult, you will need a truck or van with a smooth ramp up which the animal can be hauled (see following section).

Initial Care

Before transportation is attempted or even contemplated, it is essential to try to ascertain just why the animal is where it is. In the case of a seal, the animal may not require any help at all, although if it is an adult or a well-grown pup and has come up on a beach not normally occupied by seals, the chances are there *is* something amiss, pointing to possible sickness or injury. It may also have become badly contaminated with oil.

Typical seal

Perfectly healthy pups that have recently reached self-sufficiency may occasionally come ashore on a strange beach, having exhausted themselves in the pursuit of a meal, and very infrequently, a pup may be born and reared on such a beach.

For an inexperienced person, it is very difficult to tell whether or not a particular seal needs help. Indeed, it isn't always easy for an experienced person, so we would strongly recommend the finder to seek a second opinion before taking any action. A call to the local Fish and Wildlife Service would be a sound idea, and if it doesn't attend to it itself, it will more than likely know the right person to consult.

Likewise, in the case of a stranded whale or dolphin the Fish and Wildlife Service should be notified immediately. There are three possibilities in such a case: one, to return the animal to the sea with a minimum of stress and suffering; two, if that cannot be done for one reason or another, to let the animal die naturally if it is not suffering unduly; three, to kill it humanely if it appears to be suffering greatly.

Because the skin is thin and easily injured as well as sensitive to sun and drying, the animal should be kept moist by being splashed with sea water; take care not to splash any into the blowhole on the top of the head through which it breathes. It is simpler, if the materials are available, to cover the animal with cloths such as towels and keep these damp. If the sun should be strong, it may be possible to erect a temporary shelter over it to afford some protection. The animal must be kept upright, not lying on its side, and the flippers and tail fluke must be left free but kept damp because they are used to regulate the body temperature.

A whale or dolphin can hold its breath for anything up to fifteen minutes, and the heartbeat can rarely be heard, so it is not always a simple matter to tell if the animal is alive or dead. It also has very sensitive ears, so noisy onlookers should be kept as far away as possible.

If attempts are to be made to move the animal back to the sea, any ropes used must be well padded to prevent damage to the tender skin. If the animal is small enough, it may be possible to roll it onto a tarpaulin sheet or even a blanket and then drag or carry it, depending on the weight. To gauge the weight from the length, Lyall

Watson gives the following table:

6ft. long—about 200 lbs.
10ft.   "   —   "   1000 lbs.
13ft.   "   —   "   2000 lbs.
16ft.   "   —   "   4500 lbs.

Mass strandings are extremely difficult to deal with, and efforts to help are by no means always a success. Often there is a leader, and unless that animal is returned first, all others returned are likely to come ashore again. All the while there is one or more left on the beach, the others may try to return, presumably to try to help their fellow creatures in distress.

Food
Seals eat only fish and may devour some thrown to them. Hand feeding or force-feeding can be a hazardous business with an adult animal and should most emphatically be left to someone with experience. No attempt should be made to feed stranded whales or dolphins.

Injury and Illness
It is a comparatively rare occurrence for an adult seal to be picked up sick or injured, but such cases *do* occur. Because of the hazardous nature of dealing with such a patient and the expensive accommodation needed for convalescence, we strongly recommend that the help of some establishment specializing in marine mammals be enlisted. The same should be the case with stranded whales or dolphins.

Dolphins are susceptible to several human diseases and are particularly prone to respiratory infections.

General Care
See above.

Release
Again, this should be left to someone with experience. That person may well make the wrong decision in a given case—nobody is infallible, as anyone working in the wildlife field would readily admit—but at least the animal might have a chance of survival, and if not, it is likely to meet its end less painfully at the hands of an expert than those of a novice.

Oil Pollution

It is not uncommon for a seal's coat to become contaminated with oil, but this is by no means as serious a problem as it is for a bird. In general, nothing need be done, and the oil will simply weather off without causing the animal much problem. If the contamination is so extensive as to impair the animal's swimming ability (which in turn would deny it food), the oil can be removed in a similar manner to that described for oiled sea birds. Apart from the handling dangers, which cannot be overemphasized, the actual cleaning is easier than for a bird and need not be quite so meticulous.

Orphans

Varying methods have been employed to feed orphaned seals, ranging from tube feeding a mixture with a very high fat content to approximate mother's milk, bottle feeding with various mixtures such as a high protein/fat compound for undernourished humans, emulsified fish and whole small fish right from the start.

Although there is no very hard evidence of long-term survival after release (or at least none that has to date come to our notice), this is not to suggest that the pups do not survive. As pointed out in the oiled sea birds chapter, evidence of long-term survival of any sea creature is difficult to come by.

All the methods mentioned above seem to enjoy a measure of success as well as a measure of failure, and most people engaged in the work agree that a great deal more needs to be done for any firm conclusions to be reached.

As with adults, there is little point in an individual's attempting to rear a single pup. It is much better to send it where there are already suitable facilities and people with some prior knowledge willing to undertake the rearing. As mentioned earlier, local Fish and Wildlife Service offices, particularly those in coastal states, will almost certainly have knowledge of the nearest place which will help. And again, as suggested in the previous chapter, holding on to an animal that might have better prospects elsewhere is not only self-indulgent but not what caring for wildlife is all about.

Seals, like other animals, can easily become imprinted on humans when they have been hand-reared. Such a one came to our attention shortly before we wrote this book.

This character hauled herself ashore and just lay there, amiably surveying her surroundings and looking hopefully at any human who came into the vicinity, on the off chance he or she might have a concealed fish or two.

The local humane inspector, when he arrived on the scene, looked like just the man to provide a free meal, and the seal greeted him cordially by rolling over to have her tummy scratched prior to the expected tasty meal. But the inspector had other ideas. The seal found herself unceremoniously hauled back into the water and told, in no uncertain terms, to push off back to sea, where she belonged.

Any seal might be excused for taking umbrage at this point, but this lady was made of sterner stuff. She wasn't going to be deterred by a minor rebuff, and the next day found her once again ashore. This time, to emphasize the fact that she didn't *want* to go to sea, she climbed the riverbank, dragged herself laboriously over a large building site, over a railway line, up a very steep embankment and up onto a main road. Pausing only to catch her breath, she then set off in the general direction of the city center!

Our friend the humane inspector was going about his business, blissfully unaware of this saga, until a call came in advising him of the seal's reappearance. He set off to a given address and found her "living it up" in the flat of a friendly benefactor, where, far from reproaching the inspector for their earlier encounter, she greeted him like a long-lost friend.

Reluctantly admitting defeat, the inspector loaded her into his van and set off for home. There was obviously no point whatsoever in trying to send her out to sea when she would simply return like a boomerang and have to be picked up yet again. To prove she bore him no ill will, the seal hauled herself up from the back of the van and hung with her flippers around the inspector's neck as he drove along!

She spent the next day or two in the inspector's backyard until he could spare the time to bring her to our establishment, where better quarters could be provided. It would probably be more correct to say she was *supposed* to spend the time in the backyard, for in practice she spent it lurking by the back door and, if this should be left undone, was into the house as fast as she could go (which was quite a respectable speed when she put her mind to it).

Eventually arriving at our door, she was carried in to inspect the quarters, which consisted of one of the pools in the oiled sea bird unit (vacant at the time), to which had been added a special platform where a seal could easily haul itself out of the water. She partook of a leisurely swim, then duly hauled herself out onto the platform and went to sleep with apparent satisfaction at the turn in events. If you'll pardon the horrible pun, she seemed to have stamped her seal of approval on the new quarters.

At the time of writing, her future has not yet been decided. In the meantime, she is quite happy devouring large helpings of fish and basking in the favor of staff and public alike.

16

Medium-Sized Meat-Eaters

The species we are including in this chapter might seem diverse and arbitrary, but bear with us, for there are similarities which fit them into a group, even if the group is not a zoologically sound one.

Lined up in alphabetical order, the species concerned are: armadillo, badger, coati, opossum, raccoon, ringtail, skunk and wolverine.

Several of the species are, in fact, related. The skunk, badger and wolverine belong to the same family, as do the raccoon, ringtail and coati (though not to the same family as the first three). The opossum and armadillo are on their own zoologically speaking but are included here because, to a great extent, their care, feeding and general treatment in captivity can be virtually the same as the others.

All range in size roughly from two feet to four feet in length and most are boldly marked in one way or another. The skunks have distinctive black and white bodies and bushy tails; the badgers have black and white stripes on the head; the raccoons and relatives sport banded tails, although the banding on the coati's tail is rather indistinct and its main feature is a versatile long snout which can virtually sniff around corners. The opossum has a dark body and a light head and also has a long tail with no hair on it. The wolverine is a tough-looking thickset character, similar in appearance to a bear. In fact one of its names is skunk bear, the *skunk* part deriving from its unsavory habit of marking food (its own and other animal's) with a foul-smelling musk which only it can stand. As for the remaining group member, we would be most surprised if anyone didn't know the armadillo, in its smart suit of armor.

Possible Handling Hazards

The defensive equipment of skunks is very well known, but it can do no harm to reiterate one or two points. While the animal is facing you, there is no particular danger, although it can, and will, bite if it has to. When it reverses, however, pointing its rear end at you and raising its tail, a very rapid retreat is called for if you want the family to let you in when you get home!

Many jokes are made about it, but the smell really is atrocious, and if the spray should catch you in the eyes, the pain will be acute. Do not consider yourself safe even as much as twenty feet away, or the joke may well be on you—literally!

If you should get caught, washing clothes in soap and water will do no good whatsoever. Launder in ammonia or tomato juice. Skin exposed to the spray should be vigorously washed with carbolic soap. Ironically, the musk, which is the waxy substance left when the odor has been removed, is used in the manufacture of perfume for humans!

Raccoon

The badger is a strong animal with powerful jaws that can inflict serious injuries on the unwary human. The bite is capable of amputating a finger, and the badger has a tenacious grip which is virtually impossible to loosen without breaking the animal's jaw. In spite of this formidable equipment, the badger is not pugnacious and will bite only when very much provoked—by handling, for instance. Apart from the odd fracas with other badgers, its demeanor is amiable and non-belligerent and geared only to defense. But in defense of her cubs, a sow will fight bravely in the face of overwhelming odds and will not submit until killed.

The badger is also equipped with long, powerful claws. These are not for offense or defense, only for digging, but if you should happen to be scratched accidentally, you will certainly know about it!

Most of the above remarks apply, with equal emphasis, to the rest of the group except the armadillo, which doesn't usually bite but has even more powerful claws than the badger and can inflict painful injuries.

Approach and Capture

Some animals seem to have a positive genius for getting themselves into awkward situations. In a recent case, for instance, a badger had managed to fall into a huge tank at a sewage treatment plant. The tank was almost empty but had just sufficient unsavory sludge in the bottom to class the subsequent rescue as "beyond the call of duty"! On another occasion a cover had been left off and a badger had fallen down a fifteen-foot-deep manhole. It hadn't hurt itself but was pacing about at the bottom of the shaft, obviously annoyed. As we peered dubiously down the hole, the man who had called us asked, "Do you mind if I watch how you do it?" Note the wording of this—not "Do you think you'll be *able* to do it?" Our abilities had apparently been taken for granted as though we must surely be equipped for just such an eventuality and would say, "Ah, yes—this calls for the Acme Badger Rescue Kit Mark Two with fifteen-foot drain attachment."

The moral of these stories is that one cannot hope to be equipped for every eventuality, and improvisation is called for in most circumstances for which no simple guidelines can be drawn.

An injured and immobile member of this group, when approached, will usually crouch down with its nose to the ground and will not attempt to bite until actually touched. A dog grasper (Chapter 13) is a very useful tool. The noose can usually be eased over the head without any great objection from the animal and is usually sufficient to lift the animal into a container with the additional support of a handful of loose skin on the back near the rump. There is quite a generous amount of loose skin on the back, and lifting in this way causes no apparent discomfort. For the few seconds that all four feet are off the ground, the animal is completely disoriented and will not attempt to struggle.

Do not rely on even the thickest gloves when handling one of this group. The thickness needed to preclude any possibility of injury would also prevent any movement of the hand (which would rather defeat the object).

If no dog grasper is available, try to hold the animal's head on the ground with a thick stick until you can grasp a good handful of loose skin on the back. Then make the lift just by the skin. The operation must be executed with the utmost confidence if it is to succeed with no discomfort to the animal and no damage to the handler. If you lack this confidence (as you well may if you haven't done it before), wait until some help is available.

If there is some measure of mobility, the animal *may* be induced to enter a container of its own accord as suggested for the fox (Chapter 13), but this is somewhat unlikely with one of this group, which is apt to keep shying away from the container, using up its strength and possibly exacerbating the injury. The armadillo will normally roll itself into a ball when approached.

Transportation

A metal container such as an old metal trunk is recommended, although a wooden one would probably serve for the journey. Don't forget to make air holes. Any kind of strong cage could also be used, but a closed container is better in that the patient will prefer not to see or be seen and will travel more restfully this way.

Initial Care

Unless completely incapacitated, some of the group will not take kindly to being shut in anywhere and will employ both tooth and claw to the limit on any part of the structure that appears vulnerable and likely to afford a means of escape. In the average house there is really no place suitable to house even a semiactive badger, for instance, except a garage with metal doors, and even here it may well try to dig up a concrete floor until its claws are torn and bleeding. However, if it is essential that the animal be retained, then you can only use the best available and hope it does not fret too much with the unaccustomed confinement. Leave the traveling container as a bolt hole (it will already have gained some familiarity from the journey), tipped on its side so the patient can get in and out as it wishes, and provide food and water. Artificial heat is not necessary, and if the open end of the box faces away from any major source of draft and is close to a wall allowing just enough space for the patient to get in and out and if the box is filled with hay, this will provide sufficient comfort.

Opossum

Food

This group is not hard to please so far as food is concerned, and being shut in does not appear to adversely affect its appetite. Virtually any kind of meat will be acceptable, with canned dog or cat food the cheapest and easiest to provide. In fact, a large can of dog food mixed with dog biscuit, together with a bowl of water, will provide a perfectly satisfactory diet for the duration of the patient's stay, although it will also very much appreciate an occasional raw egg (left in the shell), a dead day-old chick or two, if you can get them, or any dead mammal or bird you may come across that has obviously been killed in a road accident. If you haven't anything else initially, a bowl of bread and milk will go down well. Several of the group, the coati in particular, are partial to fruit.

Force-feeding
Attempting to force-feed an adult is fraught with danger and is most definitely not recommended.

Symptoms, Diagnosis and Treatment
Injuries. Many of the group fall victim to road accidents and suffer wide-ranging injuries. They are also frequently caught in snares, and one researcher told us that a badger he had been tracking with a radio collar around its neck actually got caught in a snare three times during one night. It would seem that their insular attitude to life rather than any lack of intelligence accounts for this.

More often than not the animals are killed when hit by a car. Because of their size, they present a serious problem to the driver, and if the car is traveling at high speed, the collision may cause it to veer off the road, and a serious accident may result. Occasionally, however, crash injuries are not fatal to the animal. Unless injuries are slight (in which case the victim will disappear and not come to the attention of the public), the animal may be found in a dazed or shocked condition at the side of or near the road.

It is very tough, and although the injuries may look severe, it is well worth taking the animal to a veterinarian for examination and possible treatment. Broken legs can be set, and lacerations cleaned and sutured. In most cases it will be necessary to anesthetize the animal for even the simplest treatment, but nowadays this presents no real difficulty to the veterinarian.

American badger

One of the reasons this group so often gets knocked down by cars is that in its nighttime explorations and food hunts, it usually follows well-defined paths—easily visible to us in daytime—which it has trodden out over many decades of use. When a road (even a freeway) is built across one of these ancient tracks, the animal will continue to use it and amble across the road oblivious to the traffic.

It is also attracted to roads by the veritable feast of dead animals to be found in the vicinity. If it is possible without causing a hazard to following traffic, the thing to do when meeting an animal on the road at night is to stop the vehicle and turn off the headlights for a few moments to give the animal a chance to reach the roadside. It isn't just way out in the country that you might encounter one of the group by the way. We recently had brought to us a badger that had been run down on the main street of a small town.

In general, the group could be described as nature's garbage men in that it removes a good deal of refuse as it bumbles along. Any carcass it finds, be it bird, mammal, reptile or amphibian, will be eaten, as will any scraps left by picnickers, and it is by no means below its dignity to help itself from your garbage can.

Diseases. In common with all other warm-blooded mammals, this group is susceptible to rabies. Indeed, skunks are by far the commonest carriers of the disease in the United States, and while we have no wish to frighten you by exaggerating the risks of infection (which are, in fact, very low), a few details about rabies might be judicious at this point.

Skunk

The disease is caused by a fragile virus that attacks the nervous system and finally settles in the brain, where it causes serious disturbances that culminate in death, if untreated. If given in time, a vaccine will prevent it in humans. Treatment is usually successful if begun within ten to fourteen days of being bitten.

The virus is found in the saliva of an animal that is in the terminal phase of the disease and is usually transmitted by a bite. It can also enter through any broken skin or through the mucous membrane of the eye. The behavior of a severely affected animal is significantly altered, making it far less afraid of humans and much more aggressive.

At one time 80 percent of all cases of rabies in the United States occurred in dogs. Now, however, vaccination has successfully protected them, and the majority of animals dying of the disease are wild (skunks, foxes, etc.). Nearly all cases of rabies in livestock can be traced to rabid wild animals. The number of human beings dying of rabies is very small indeed (five in the period

1962–65). If you should be bitten by any animal, it should be retained if at all possible for observation and examination, and your doctor should be advised.

Diseases such as distemper, leptospirosis and Rocky Mountain spotted fever are known to exist in this group of animals, and it is believed that the raccoon acts as a carrier (i.e., a potential source of infection for other species without being seriously affected itself) for several diseases, such as vesicular stomatitis, mink virus enteritis, feline panleukopenia and histoplasmosis.

There is insufficient space to probe deeply into these or other diseases affecting the group. They don't make for cheery reading and are really a matter for your veterinarian. Still, there is just one small item which might be of interest. Some free-living armadillos have recently been found to be affected by leprosy, and they have also been found to be susceptible to a number of other human diseases. This fact is most unfortunate for them because they are now used widely in laboratories, both for this reason and for the fact that they produce identical offspring.

General Care

An outside pen for a wild adult is not an easy or cheap item to provide. Like the fox (Chapter 13), this group is good at both climbing and digging. In climbing ability it probably matches the fox, but in digging, this group is undoubtedly superior, and while the general principles of the pen described in Chapter 13 would apply, one or two modifications are advisable for complete security.

In the early stages of being incarcerated in the pen, some are apt to bite and worry at the wire itself, even making their mouths bleed. A fence of only 16 gauge may not break, but it would certainly become very distorted by this attention, and 12 or even 10 gauge is recommended. The ground wire in the pen should be placed some distance underground, allowing the animal to do a certain amount of digging. The wire should cover the whole of the pen area since the animal may commence excavations at any point, very often under its sleeping quarters. Depending on the nature of the ground, it can dig quite an appreciable length of tunnel in one night. Just how far underground the base wire is placed depends entirely on how much you yourself want to do or have done. About twelve to eighteen inches would be fine.

If you can provide a sleeping box which can be closed (e.g., a channel for a sliding door [see fig. 15, page 128]), this will help considerably when the time comes for release. By this time your guest won't be at all easy to catch or handle.

Release

All being well, the animal should be asleep in its box when you slide the door into place. Without pain to either side, both animal and box can be transported to the point of release—preferably as near as possible to the point where it was found, enabling the animal to return to its home den. If the release is made at dusk, the sliding door can be removed and the animal tipped out unceremoniously. It won't protest at this undignified exit and will almost certainly lope off immediately in the direction of home.

If it is impossible for some reason to return the animal to its home ground, your local Fish and Wildlife Service office should be able to assist in selecting a suitable spot.

Orphans

It is an exceptional circumstance that will bring in youngsters less than about six weeks old, for this is the very youngest they are likely to be abroad of their own accord. Even then, they are unlikely to move far from the den entrance, where they can bolt back at the first hint of disturbance. If an infant should be found on its own, the chances are it will be over three months old, in which case it should be able to feed itself. Suckling opossums may be found clinging to a dead mother.

On one or two occasions we have had young badger cubs brought in, and these have been reared in the same manner and on the same mixture as for fox cubs (see Chapter 13), but a baby's bottle with a premature baby's teat is used instead of the syringe. Bottle feeding continues until the cubs are just over three months old, but we reduce it in the latter stages, with only two bottle feedings a day in the final week. This formula and frequency should be satisfactory for most of the group, although we cannot claim personal experience. For very small opossums, the recommended formula would undoubtedly be too strong, although the same formula at half strength may well do the trick.

In the absence of a mother, infants are apt to try to suckle from any male sibling, on a sensitive part of his anatomy which can be made quite sore. Watch for this happening, and separate them if necessary.

A move into a pen outside can be made before the end of weaning (at about eight or nine weeks), as described for adult casualties. A portable den should again be provided, unless the youngster can be released directly from the pen into a suitable locality, in which case a burrow more resembling a natural den can be provided. If the cubs cannot be so released, a good deal of thought must go into just where they are placed; seek all possible advice, and do not release them too early (about five months minimum). They must be strong enough and large enough to have a reasonable chance with any possible adversary they might encounter. With the permission of the owner, it might be possible to construct an artificial den in a piece of woodland not already occupied, which would help very much in giving them a good start. Of course, there is no guarantee they would stay there, but *any* release to the wild of a hand-reared youngster is a risk. As someone once said in a different context, "If you put up too many fences against the risks, you end by shutting out life itself."

Hand-reared young of this group make an easier transition than many from a sheltered existence to a wild one, and the change to a nocturnal way of life seems quite effortless and can happen suddenly. One day they will be puttering about in broad daylight, and then, just as though a switch had been thrown, they may never be seen again during the day. We recall one particular young badger called Hazel, one of three brought in at about three months old. The parents had been found dead on a road, and the three youngsters were found on the verge nearby. It was some time before they were brought to us, and one was very weak on arrival and died overnight. A second went to another home. This left Hazel, who was bottle-fed for a week or so before she would deign to feed herself. We allowed her the freedom of the premises, and when she began to get out and about, she struck up a friendship with a lamb that had also been hand-reared. They used to spend all day together nosing around or rough-housing. It was quite hilarious to watch Hazel taking a sudden nip at the lamb's foot, then setting off as fast as she could go, with the lamb bouncing along like a rubber ball behind her.

After a time the lamb was transferred elsewhere, leaving Hazel to putter about on her own. During one particular day's explorations she found her way under a large shed. She stayed there for quite a time, and when she finally emerged, it was to spend the rest of the day carrying her bedding from where she had been living to her new home under the shed. We watched these operations with interest. The furniture removal was completed by about midafternoon, at which time Hazel disappeared under the shed and was never again seen in daylight. She lived there for some time before finally making her way into the countryside, where we hope she survived. From reports received subsequently, we know she was still living a year afterward.

17

Deer and Pronghorn

Cloven-footed animals range in size from very small (relatively) to very large. In fact, some of the largest animals in North America belong to this group. There are a number of interesting species, but we will confine ourselves to the deer and the pronghorn, which, apart from the dwarf deer, are by far the most common of the group in the United States.

White-tailed deer, once almost exterminated, are now the most common game animal in the United States—thanks to laws regulating hunting. At an average weight of 250 pounds the male is one-third bigger than the female. Only the males have antlers. These begin growing in the spring and are covered with soft skin bearing short, velvetlike hairs, hence the reason for the phrase *in velvet* (the time when the antlers are growing). Well supplied with blood vessels, this skin is easily damaged and will bleed. In New Zealand this velvet is harvested by either killing the deer or simply catching it, cutting off the antlers and then peeling off the velvet skin. And the reason is a lucrative trade, principally to the Far East, where it is used as an aphrodisiac. Analysis has shown that the skin does, in fact, contain small amounts of the male hormone testosterone, which incidentally can be obtained from other sources much more cheaply. It can be synthesized, for example, but folklore has a strong appeal.

At the end of the summer the antlers are fully grown, and the blood supply, controlled by hormones, is cut off. The skin dies and peels off in flakes, leaving the bare antlers, which last until after the mating season. Each year the antlers are bigger, and in some species (not white-tailed deer) the stag's age can be determined by the number of branches or points on the antlers.

White-tailed deer graze on green plants and browse

on nuts and woody vegetation, mostly at night, but by no means always. If alarmed, the deer raises its tail, exposing the white rump, which bobs up and down as it runs, thus signaling danger to the others.

Mule deer are found in the western United States and are similar in appearance to the white-tail. Their coat is less reddish and more the color of a donkey, and their ears are bigger. They will eat crops and bark off young growing trees and when numerous in an area, can do a lot of damage.

The pronghorn is the only American antelope. It is smaller than the mule deer, weighing about 100 pounds, and its coat is reddish brown. The males have short, pronged horns, which are shed a month after breeding, in the fall. The young fawns are born in May. The fawns are odorless and lie quiet and apparently abandoned for about a week. The mother returns to them only to feed them so as to avoid attracting predators. Once their numbers got as low as 20,000, but now management measures have brought the total population to about 500,000. It is the fastest animal in America, and a speed of 70 mph has been recorded.

The tiny coues deer and key deer are actually subspecies of the white-tail. Their range is very limited, the coues to the desert of Arizona and the key, as its name implies, to the Florida Keys, where it is fully protected.

White-tailed deer

The fallow deer, also confined to localized areas dotted about the country, is actually an imported Old World species living both wild and in semidomesticated herds. A beautiful animal, it can be distinguished by the palmated antlers of the male.

Possible Handling Hazards

The handling of deer by inexperienced people alone, particularly the larger species, is not recommended. The trouble is that most people are apt to be imbued with the gentle and delicate "Bambi" image of deer, whereas the hoof of a large deer can disembowel, and we have seen severe facial lacerations, almost removing an eye, caused by a fallow deer with only three legs.

In most areas where deer are present, there is someone with experience who will attend to a casualty, and the local police or Fish and Wildlife officer will doubtless know where he or she is to be found. We strongly urge you to call upon such a person when you encounter an injured deer. The following notes should be acted upon only if there is absolutely *no* help available or forthcoming.

Approach and Capture

If the deer is on its feet, it will probably run away when approached, although a male *may* launch an attack, particularly during the mating season (in the fall). In a confined situation, *any* deer may try to fend off what it considers an attack. With the female, this will take the form of rearing on her hindlegs and "boxing" with her front hooves, while a male will usually attack with the head, whether equipped with antlers or not. In such a situation, tranquilization by darting may well be called for, and this is definitely a job for the expert (see "Symptoms, Diagnosis and Treatment"). Deer do not bite.

If the animal is lying down, try to keep its head on the ground, cushioning it with a coat, but keep well clear of the hooves until it is time for the move.

Transportation

Before moving the patient, it may be desirable to hobble it—to tie its legs loosely together to prevent it from rising—and again we must reiterate the warning: Do not underestimate the strength of what appear to be slender, delicate legs, or you may lose an eye. If it is a male, the antlers will have to be protected or, in some cases, removed by an expert. In the case of a pricket (second-year male), when there is simply a spike with no tines (branching spikes), a piece of hose can be slipped over each or a piece of sacking can be tied around each. In the case of a mature male in velvet, no attempt should be made to remove the antlers, but they must be protected with lots of padding on each (with wooden splints on each antler) and *between* the antlers. At other times the antlers are in effect dead, and no pain or adverse effect is caused by removing them. The cut is best made above the brow tine (the first spike which sticks out to the front), preferably using an embryotomy wire, which any veterinarian will have among his or her equipment (although a saw can be used).

A minimum floor area in the vehicle of about 2 × 4 feet will be required to transport a white-tail, and it may require four people to lift the animal.

Initial Care

In our experience, wild adult deer do not like to be inside a building. They appear to suffer severely from claustrophobia, and this may be a contributing factor to the death of a casualty so kept. An open paddock with plenty of undergrowth or a few bales of straw to screen the animal from view is preferable. In the case of a patient that cannot move, some kind of awning should be rigged to protect it from heavy rain (which it will be unable to shake off), or it should be placed under a tree with plenty of foliage, which will serve the same purpose. Some water should be administered, and this can be done quite easily; dribble it into the mouth with the aid of a plastic syringe and give a generous quantity—up to half a pint for a white-tail. Of course, if the animal will drink by itself, there is no need for administration, but an initial intake of liquid, one way or the other, will undoubtedly be beneficial. A bowl of water should also be left within easy reach, and some food provided.

Mule
deer (male)

Food

If you can get hold of some, ivy will tempt the appetite of most deer. Rose petals also seem to be palatable, and other suitable foods include the leaves of broad-leafed trees, grass, hay, root and leaf vegetables, nut kernels, chick pellets and cereals. One deer of our acquaintance is very fond of canned fish in tomato sauce!

In general, a deer casualty's willingness to take nourishment is a good pointer to the severity of its injury. In other words, if it refuses to feed voluntarily, its chances of ultimate recovery are slim.

Force-feeding

Force-feeding is a fairly easy task and can be undertaken if it is thought desirable. But always bear in mind the dangers outlined previously. A plastic syringe can be used, although it will need to be filled a good many times at each feeding in order to give sufficient nourishment, particularly to the larger species, which will require at least 1 pint (600 milliliters) two or three times a day. An empty dishwashing liquid bottle can be used, and the food can be squeezed into the side of the mouth directly from this. Use a baby cereal at the thickest it will come out of the container, or Esbilac. And do not rush it, allow the animal plenty of time to swallow the mixture.

Symptoms, Diagnosis and Treatment

Injuries. In common with many other animals, deer fall victim of road accidents, with broken legs or dislocated limbs as the principal injuries, together with abrasions and lacerations of the skin. Occasionally they get caught in snares, and one recent sufferer we saw had to be shot. The snare had tightened around the animal's neck and must have finally broken it after lacerating the skin. It had occurred several weeks earlier, for the skin was beginning to grow over the wire as it encircled the neck. The windpipe had been partly severed, and the animal was breathing through the hole in its neck as well as through its mouth. This obviously greatly impaired its ability to get about, and it was seen to be trailing behind the family group, often standing on its own. For this reason it was singled out and caught. The snare — not visible from a distance because of the skin growing over it — was found and the animal shot. The injuries were so severe that it would have caused a considerable amount of suffering to have attempted to treat the animal. A horrific example of man's inhumanity to animal.

Fallow

It is not uncommon to find deer trapped in wire fencing (apart from wire snares). The animal may have attempted to jump over or through the fence and got stuck. Sometimes the wire breaks and a portion remains wrapped around a leg.

The wisest course of action is to mark the spot carefully and seek help as quickly as possible. Deer are easily frightened, especially when caught in wire, and may cause themselves much more serious injuries when approached. If the animal is exhausted, it may be approached slowly and carefully and then held firmly while the wire is cut away. Otherwise it should be darted with a tranquilizer, and this means the assistance of a veterinarian. The tranquilizer used is a powerful drug, called etorphine (M99), that has an antidote. The dart must be loaded with the correct dose according to the weight of the animal and fired into the muscle (usually the rump). It is absorbed and acts within ten to fifteen minutes. After being hit, the animal runs away, slows down gradually, staggers and falls. It can then be secured and given the antidote.

Not infrequently deer are involved in motorcar accidents—a hazard not only to themselves but to human beings as well. For example, in New York State 20,000 deer are killed annually. Recently an Austrian company developed an ultrasonic warning device which has worked well in both Austria and Finland. It consists of a pair of two-inch sound tubes which produce, at 30 mph or more, an ultrasonic sound that can be heard by the deer but not by humans. Another device developed in Austria consists of red reflectors along the road which reflect the cars' headlights and scare the deer. Already it is being used in the United States and Canada.

Occasionally in certain areas deer have been found with heads of arrows from crossbows sticking in them. The animal has to be caught, tranquilized, and the arrowhead removed—which, of course, requires the services of a veterinarian. Gunshot wounds from hunters are not uncommon, and again help should be sought to catch and treat the animal.

Peruke head (from the French, meaning a wig) is the abnormal grotesque growth of velvet antler as a result of damage to the testicles by either injury or castration. This stops the production of the sex hormone testosterone, which controls the antler growth cycle. This abnormal growth is seen on deer with some new growth each summer adding to the antler growth which is never shed. Because it remains in velvet, the growth is susceptible to damage and hemorrhage, for the velvet covering the growth is really skin amply supplied with blood vessels.

If a young deer under nine months of age is castrated, the pedicle from which the antler normally grows never forms, and the deer will never grow antlers throughout his life. If castration or severe damage occurs to an adult stag while he is in velvet, growth continues for a while and finally ceases. If castration or severe damage occurs to an adult stag with hard antlers, they are immediately shed (within three weeks) and growth commences at once. But the antlers never reach their proper size and shape, though they grow for a longer time, and they remain in velvet and never harden.

Diseases and Poisoning. Deer usually appear fairly healthy, but this is not uncommon with wild animals. In spite of this, they suffer from a variety of diseases, including tuberculosis, foot-and-mouth disease, cancer and both internal and external parasites.

Actinomycosis is a chronic infection of the jawbone, causing swelling. It has been diagnosed in both white-tailed and mule deer. Anaplasmosis, a disease of the blood, has also been found in deer. It is transmitted by blood-sucking insects and causes serious anemia because of the destruction of the red blood cells. Anthrax, a serious infection which can affect humans, has also been diagnosed in deer. It generally manifests itself in humans either through the outbreak of cutaneous pustules or pulmonary infection. Foot-and-mouth disease will affect deer, and in 1924, 22,000 deer were killed in an attempt to eradicate the disease. Another infection which will attack humans and is found in deer and other ruminants is listerellosis, which causes many small abscesses in the brain. On one occasion the daughter of a farmer was taken to a hospital with a fever and nervous symptoms, derangement of balance and headaches. The doctors were nonplussed, and her head was shaved for an exploratory examination. The farmer then told the author that while some calves were being treated for listerellosis, the child had been playing with the sick calves. The hospital was informed, and the correct treatment was given. She rapidly recovered.

Deer also suffer occasionally from tumors — often skin cancer. A large number of diseases affect this group, but none is really common. And the records are more an indication of the extensive investigations carried out than the extent of the problem. It certainly does not mean that deer are unhealthier than other mammals. But of course, the longer the animal lives, the more opportunity there is of contracting disease.

When an animal becomes diseased or old and debilitated in the wild, it falls easy prey to predators. This may seem cruel, but it terminates quickly, although traumatically, an otherwise lengthy period of suffering. Prey animals must show no signs of weakness to predators lest they be singled out, and for this reason disease is often fairly advanced before the animal allows the symptoms to show. It is, therefore, possible that members of the public, while walking in the countryside, may come across a deer that is disinclined to move, is perhaps unsteady on its feet and looks thin (though often a heavy coat hides the real condition of the animal). Emaciation causes wasting of the facial muscles and a depletion of the fat behind and around the eye. This causes the eye to sink to the socket, immediately obvious. Such cases should be reported to the Fish and Wildlife Service. The cause could be any one of those mentioned above, and an examination by a veterinarian is required.

General Care

If a deer is to be kept for any length of time, it must have a paddock of adequate size so that the area does not become totally contaminated with droppings, which is a hazard to the animal's health. To house a single white-tail on a long-term basis, we would recommend an area not less than 50 × 25 yards. The paddock should be enclosed by a six-foot-high fence, which can be of sheep netting and should include some shelter from wind, which deer do not seem to like very much, and from sun. Shelter from rain and other elements is not necessary for a fit or reasonably fit animal but is needed for an immobile patient (see page 162). Bear in mind that any trees, shrubs or plants within the boundary are likely to suffer grievous bodily harm!

Do not expect the natural contents of the paddock to sustain the deer. Continue to provide food from the list given. We generally give a type of cattle mix usually called dairy mixture, some chick pellets and peanut kernels as a regular diet, supplemented with other tidbits from time to time.

Pronghorn

Orphans

A good many deer picked up as orphans are not really orphans at all. The doe will leave her youngster(s) hiding in the grass while she grazes in the vicinity. The fawn(s) will not move at any approach, and of course, they are found apparently alone and "lost" when the mother will, in fact, be watching from somewhere very close by. Anyone needing reassurance of this point should note the spot where they have seen the youngster and leave without touching it at all, returning an hour or so later to see if it is still there. The chances are it won't be. If it is, then there *is* some reason to wonder, particularly if the youngster is by this time making peeping noises indicating distress.

There are, of course, many circumstances producing quite genuine orphans, such as hunters killing the mother or, as in a recent case we had, the mother being killed by a vehicle, leaving twin fawns sitting dutifully by her dead body, waiting for her to show them what to do next. In these circumstances the youngster must obviously be taken into care, but more often than not, this will change the whole course of their lives. It is very difficult to keep a young deer from becoming imprinted on the person feeding it and to lose its fear of other humans—a fatal affliction for any wild animal.

If you find more than one deer at the same time, there is a better chance of a "wild rearing." We have reared a number of pairs and been able to release them to the wild, whereas most hand-reared single deer have to go to some sheltered environment.

Unlike the case of adult casualties, it is safe and indeed desirable to keep the youngsters indoors for a time, at least until they are well accustomed to accepting the bottle from you. If placed out of doors from the start, they will simply tear around in a blind panic at your approach.

We always use Esbilac for feeding young deer (see Appendix C). Whatever you start to use, stick with it for the duration of the weaning; otherwise you will certainly encounter problems or even flat rejection of the new food when you try to change over. Ordinary cows' milk is not suitable.

A maximum of five feedings per day is sufficient for even the very youngest, but the actual quantity will vary considerably, depending on the species. A key deer, for instance, will start at about five fluid ounces, and a white-tail will take about fifteen fluid ounces. These quantities should be increased as the youngster manages to empty the bottle easily. You cannot overfeed, for the infant will simply stop sucking when it has had enough, but time must be allowed during a feeding for the odd scamper about.

An ordinary baby's feeding bottle is fine for deer up to key size, but the larger species need more than eight fluid ounces at a "sitting." An ordinary pint soft-drink bottle with a calf teat attached can be used. Calf teats are available from a dairy farmer's supplier.

We have frequently found that young deer taken out for a short stroll after feeding will eat a bit of soil. Whether this is of any great significance is hard to say, but we now always keep a bowl of soil in the pen so that they can help themselves should they wish. A selection of solid food should also be offered from an early stage. The youngsters like to try nibbling at various items.

Milk feedings will need to be continued until the youngster is at least four months old, although when the change can be made from drinking out of a bottle to out of a bowl or bucket is an individual matter, not even one of species. We have had some (of various species) drinking from a bowl or bucket as early as one month and some that would not even try until at least a month later.

There is also no hard-and-fast rule for the move out of doors. As indicated earlier, we make this move as soon as the youngsters have an established feeding pattern and no longer shy away when their foster mom comes to feed them. In this respect, it is by far best if one person undertakes the whole of the bottle feeding.

A paddock, as described for adult casualties, should be provided with the added refinement of an open-fronted box of sufficient size for the species (and numbers) concerned, furnished with straw for bedding. Young deer will usually use such a sleeping box if it is provided, but if they simply bed down under a bush, don't worry about it.

If it hasn't finished drinking the formula by four months of age, start diluting the feeds (which should be no more than one a day by this time) until they are simply water and the youngster gets the message.

Release may present a great problem, as indicated earlier. If the youngster is so tame that it has completely lost its natural timidity, the chances are that it will walk up to the first person who comes along. That person might be the wrong one, and the fruit of your labor might be knocked on the head and wind up in a Deep-freeze. If you have been skillful (or lucky) and the animal runs away when approached—at least from other people—then by all means try a release in an area already frequented by the particular species. If it shows *no* fear, then the only course is to find a home for it in some private park. Your local Fish and Wildlife Service may be able to help place the animal.

Mammal Addendum

There are a number of species we haven't included. This is not because they are tiny, insignificant creatures; on the contrary, most of those left out are large and spectacular, such as the bears, for instance.

Why have we left them out? Well, for one reason, we haven't enough personal experience of any of them to give much detail, and for another, you are unlikely ever to have to deal with any of them, although it is by no means unknown for a motorist to "find" a bear cub and take it home.

Another very sound reason for not including the remaining mammal species in a book on animal care and handling is that most of those not included are highly dangerous and definitely should not be approached by a layperson. It would not be an exaggeration to say that an inexperienced person trying any care and handling could well wind up dead!

PART THREE

OTHER WILDLIFE

18

Snakes, Lizards and Turtles

Very few people will ever have the opportunity of giving assistance to the sick and injured creatures covered in this and the following two chapters. But if ill treatment is prevented, their inclusion in this book will have been justified.

There are 115 species of snakes in America, and most are rarely seen by the public. Even so, they usually evoke fear in spite of the fact that if left alone, they will retreat. However, 19 species are venomous and should be given due respect.

Snakes are cold-blooded. This does not mean that their blood is cold—indeed, if it were, the animals would be comatose or at least very lethargic—but that they are unable to produce body heat wholly by metabolic processes and control their temperature as accurately as mammals do. Snakes rely instead on the sun to warm them into activity, and they must hibernate in the winter months.

They have an outer skin of scales and no skin glands, so that contrary to popular belief, snakes are dry to the touch. They cannot sweat since, apart from having no skin glands, they have an outer layer of transparent skin over the top of the scales. This covers even their eyes, so that tears have to escape through the nostrils.

On average they have 150 vertebrae, each carrying two ribs all the way to the vent (no breastbone), and then a further 50 vertebrae without ribs in the tail. Their teeth are not in their jaws but in a number of bars running lengthways in the mouth. They have neither eyelids nor ears, so are deaf to sight and sound, but are highly sensitive to vibrations. The tongue is the sensitive organ of touch.

The majority of species of venomous snakes are found in the southern half of the United States. The important exceptions are the four-foot-long copperhead, found from southwestern Massachusetts down to Florida, and the six-foot-long timber and western rattlesnakes, which are found as far north as Maine and the Canadian border respectively. They all are members of the pit viper family. Other important members of this family are the cottonmouth, whose bite can be fatal, and the eastern diamondback rattlesnake, which is the most dangerous snake in America. Rattlesnakes have a series of flattened dry segments, formed when they shed their skins, joined together on their tails, and these produce a buzzing, rattling sound when shaken.

The other important poisonous snake is from another family—the eastern coral or the scarlet king snake—and is only found as far north as North Carolina.

The most widely distributed snake in America is the harmless common garter snake. Up to four feet in length, it is to be found in damp areas from sea level to 8,000 feet. It gives birth to its young rather than lays eggs. Another very common snake is the larger rat snake, up to 8 feet long; it is a powerful constrictor. The racer, on the other hand, is slender and not quite so long and is found in every state except Alaska.

Rat snake

The most common aquatic snake is the northern water snake, which feeds mainly on fish. When surprised, it will flee, but if cornered, it will strike, and because of an anticoagulant in its saliva, wounds will bleed profusely.

Racer

The eastern hognose snake and the pine-gopher, on the other hand, will attack if confronted, though they rarely bite human beings.

The 3,000 or so species of lizards in the world today make them the largest group of reptiles. They vary in size, color and shape, more than any other group. America has 115. Only one, the gila monster, is poisonous.

Lizards, which superficially resemble salamanders, have dry skins and external ear openings. Most, but not all, have legs and clawed feet and movable eyelids. The legless lizards look like snakes but have movable eyelids. All are cold-blooded, and most hibernate in the winter months and are active in moderate heat. High midday temperatures make them rest, for too high a body temperature is as dangerous as too low.

Eastern lizard (broken-striped)

There are ten species of gecko in America, only five

*Eastern glass
lizard*

*Six-lined
race runner*

*Five-lined
skink*

Gila monster

Iguana

of which are native. They are the smallest lizards, and the tiny suction cups on the ends of the bristles on their pads permit them to walk up walls and across ceilings. They are active at night, and their large eyes have no eyelids. Their tails are brittle and easily break off, often, it seems, when only touched. And their skin is fragile and easily damaged.

Whiptails, of which there are seventeen species in the United States, are long, slender lizards with long tails. They eat insects and, if they are large enough, consume small mammals, birds and other reptiles. A single family consists of several species that breed unisexually—that is to say, all are females, none is male, so there is no mating.

Let us pass quickly on to the skinks, of which there are fifteen species in the United States. These resemble whiptail lizards but are longer and sleeker and have small legs.

Large-bodied lizards of the iguana family have forty-four species in the United States. They vary considerably in appearance and size, and typically they have five-toed feet on all four legs. Most feed on insects. They are bisexual, and both courting and aggression are commonly seen, though the aggression displays almost never end in fights. They content themselves with jousting or just displays of head bobbing, mouth opening and tail curling—not entirely unknown in the human political arena.

Two should be mentioned in particular—the gila monster and the desert iguana. The former is the only poisonous lizard in the United States. The gila monster is a formidable one and a half to two feet long. Its poison comes from glands along the inside of the lower jaw. This is not injected but flows into the ragged wound made by the repeated gnawing of jaws which never let go. The effect is painful but not fatal.

The desert iguana is only one foot long and rather nervous. It can be seen in southern California and neighboring states, generally fleeing at your approach. Because desert iguanas tolerate high temperatures, they can often be seen at a distance, basking on the rocks.

The final group of reptiles to be mentioned here are the turtles. The United States has three species of soft-shelled turtles. The largest, the Florida softshell, is about one foot long. The smooth softshell is smaller and is found in nearly every river of the Mississippi waterway. The spiny softshell is to be found in the southeastern states. All are fast swimmers and will rarely be found injured or diseased.

Box turtle

The box turtles (of which there are twenty-six species in the United States) are semiaquatic and herbivorous. They also will be rarely found in trouble.

There are only three species of snapping turtles, and they are the largest of fresh-water turtles. They have large heads and powerful jaws. They are found in all states except the western. The alligator snapping turtle is the largest fresh-water turtle in the world, weighing up to 200 pounds.

Snapping turtle

Five species of sea turtle are found around the coast, and all are endangered: the loggerhead in the Atlantic and the Pacific, which can weigh up to 600 pounds; the green turtle, with a similar range and size; the hawksbill, smaller but with the same range; the Atlantic ridley, also smaller and found along the Atlantic coast; and the olive ridley, a fish-eating species found in the warmer waters of the Atlantic and Pacific.

Green turtle

Possible Handling Hazards

Many of the creatures in this group can, and will, bite if cornered or handled. However, because of their size, none of the bites is likely to be serious, though they will undoubtedly be painful. But the bites of the poisonous snakes and the poisonous lizard can be life-threatening, especially to children, and even the treatment is not without risks.

More than 7,000 Americans are bitten each year, and the most dangerous bites are caused by rattlesnakes and copperheads. Their poison damages tissue around the bite and enters the bloodstream, causing internal hemorrhage and attacking the nervous system. This affects respiration and induces convulsions. There are two methods of treatment, and both should be employed as soon as possible after being bitten—every minute counts. Many doctors give antivenin serum to neutralize the poison, but because it is a protein itself, it can, and often does, cause allergic reactions, which can be as mild as skin swellings (hives) or as severe as feverlike symptoms that may in some cases be as dangerous as the snake venom itself. A doctor should have drugs on hand to combat these reactions. The other method is to pack

Timber rattlesnake

the area around the bite with ice to shut down the blood vessels and prevent the poison from spreading. Then the doctor will remove surgically all damaged tissue and wash away the poison. There is no doubt that the effect of the poison on the tissue around the wound can be severe, and patients given serum sometimes recover from the life-threatening effects of the nervous and circulatory system only to face the possibility of a massive wound or even amputation. The success of this method depends on getting to the doctor before the poison can spread.

Of course, it should be remembered that the poisonous snake does not always inject poison. So what does one do?

Remain Calm.

Put ice on and around the bite.

Go as fast as possible to the doctor.

Take the snake with you (if it is dead) for identification. And if it has disappeared, make a mental note of what it looked like, unless you know the species, of course. Only if you are far from a doctor should the bite be cut open and the poison sucked out.

Bites aside, strange, unforeseen accidents can happen with the animals mentioned in this chapter. A giant tortoise weighing more than 200 pounds was brought for examination and treatment. It had a damaged eye, and while it was feeding on a piece of banana, Bill grabbed its head. But it was far stronger than he, and retracting its head inside its shell, it drew his hand in rapidly. Unfortunately there wasn't quite room enough for both of them. Bill's knuckles had the skin scraped off and it was all he could do to retrieve his hand. Now what to do? The problem was solved by luck, for when the giant was tipped onto its tail with head end pointing skyward, its head popped out, presumably to keep its balance, and Bill could proceed without further trouble.

Approach and Capture

No attempts should be made to approach and capture an animal of this group unless it is obviously injured and can be helped or unless it has to be moved for its own safety or that of human beings.

The simplest way to catch a snake or lizard is with a catching net (see fig. 1, page 4). Once in the net, it can be transferred to a cotton bag.

Transportation
The snake or lizard can be carried in a cotton bag, which can be placed in a box if necessary.

Initial Care
Rest and quiet in a covered ventilated box with sand on the floor, a temperature of 71° to 77° F (22° to 25° C) and drinking water are the important points. Reptiles will not usually feed in this initial stage of their captivity.

Food
Snakes will not normally feed in captivity to begin with and may well be ready for release before they are settled enough to try. They don't eat regularly, and fasting will not be a problem to them. Lizards, on the other hand, will usually feed if kept quiet and undisturbed, though they can also safely go without food if insects cannot be obtained for them.

Symptoms, Diagnosis and Treatment
Like all other animals, reptiles can be injured and suffer from disease. Injuries can be accidental, such as being run over by a car or stepped on by an animal. They should be humanely put to sleep if the injuries seem extensive. But remember that the slowworm and the other lizards can and do lose their tails without suffering even shock in the process. Snakes, on the other hand, do not have brittle tails, and injuries should be treated. If the wound is kept clean, it will generally heal fairly rapidly.

It is extremely difficult for the expert and impossible for the layperson to diagnose disease in reptiles. They show no consistent recognizable symptoms except loss of weight or diarrhea, and diagnosis must usually be made on postmortem examination. Even if the reptile looks ill, leave it alone.

General Care
The aim must be to cure the animal as quickly as possible. Once a wound is healing well, the snake can be safely released. Any kind of smooth-sided box or an empty aquarium with sand on the bottom will serve for convalescence. Keep in a fairly warm room—(about 77° F (25° C)—with water always available.

Release

It is best to release the reptile where it was found if possible, for it will know the area and will have more chance of survival.

An amusing footnote: Not long ago a lady brought a land tortoise to me because she said it was ill. She placed it on the table. Bill fingered his stethoscope, not knowing what to do, for it sat in its shell impassively. "How do you know it's ill?" Bill ventured. "Has it shown any symptoms you can describe?"

"No," she said, "except that it just doesn't come when I call its name anymore." Now I'm in trouble, Bill thought.

"Well, try calling it now," he suggested.

She did, and a little head popped out and looked around, searching for the sound. Then four legs appeared, and the tortoise slowly raised itself and staggered toward the owner. Do all reptiles have the capability of responding as this one did? Bill wondered. Incidentally, he gave it a shot of vitamins, and it recovered its former dash and charm.

Reptile Addendum

As with the mammals, there are some formidable reptiles we haven't included—namely, the crocodilians, which are to be found only in the southern states, e.g., Florida, South Texas, and southern Arkansas, Oklahoma and North Carolina.

There are three species, with only the largest, the American alligator, to be found over all of the above range. The other two are the American crocodile and the spectacled caiman, which was originally imported for the pet trade!

As with those in the mammal addendum, these animals are definitely not for handling by the amateur. They may *look* as though they're smiling, but don't you believe it!

19

Amphibia

Amphibia are more primitive creatures than reptiles. Frogs and toads have nine vertebrae (but no ribs) and a three-chambered heart. In spite of the fact that their skin is smooth and moist and contains a great number of glands, they do not produce the same nervousness in human beings that snakes or even lizards do. Glands in their skin contain different pigments which can be squeezed to drive the color to the surface, thus enabling the animal to match its color to its surroundings. They have many predators, and changing color is one of their major protective mechanisms. The toad has another talent, not shared by common frogs or newts: Its skin is covered with glands that give out an irritant poison when it is roughly handled. This poison will not penetrate the human skin but will irritate the mucous lining of the mouth and eye. No dog that has ever picked up a toad will do so again. It will quickly drop the toad and will go off, shaking its head and working its tongue to get rid of the irritation.

Spotted salamander

With neither ribs nor diaphragm, breathing is done by the throat. The frog or toad closes its mouth and nostrils and forces air down into the lungs. It does this at quite a fast rate, but if you look carefully, you can see the underneath part of the throat pulsating. During hibernation in winter, oxygen is absorbed through the pores all over the skin and mouth so that breathing as such is unnecessary.

The long, slender body of the salamander superficially resembles a lizard, and the salamander is sometimes mistaken for a lizard. But on closer examination one can see that the salamander has a moist skin with no scales, no claws and no external ear openings.

There are eighteen species of toad native to the United States. The Woodhouse's and the American toad are the ones usually seen. The natterjack toad is endangered. These toads are friends of the gardener, for they have an insatiable appetite for slugs, caterpillars, beetles and other insects. Like reptiles, they shed their skins every few weeks as they grow. The skin splits down the back and gradually peels off, a process which toads help along with their hands and feet. Toads' move slowly with a sort of crawl or short, heavy hops. In fact, everything about them is slow except their large, flat, sticky, elastic tongues which can be flicked out rapidly for about two inches (five centimeters) to catch their prey.

American toad

Most toads are adept burrowers. They rest during the day, for they are active at night, feeding on insects. The giant toad has become adapted to gardens, and it will quickly accept food offered in the hand. Toads consume large numbers of garden and agricultural pests and can truly be called friends.

In the spring they head for ponds to mate and attract each other with croaking and whining bleats. The males embrace the willing females and remain locked for a week or more. The females produce several hundred eggs in strings which trail around the water weeds in the pond. They hatch into tiny black tadpoles, which reach their maximum size in seventy days. After a further fifteen days the tadpole metamorphosises into a minute toad, which swims to the shore. Many are taken by predators, and the lucky ones take about five years to reach maturity.

There are twenty-one species of true frogs, together with one species of tailed frog, three narrow-mouthed frog species and twenty-six species of tree frogs in the United States. True frogs are large with long legs and are excellent jumpers. They are more truly amphibious in that they are in and out of the pond water daily. Their mating habits are similar to toads, but the female lays many more eggs—up to 20,000.

Bull frog

Tree frogs are small with thin legs and sticky adhesive pads on their toes. The northern cricket frog is perhaps the most common and is found in most states. It has a shrill clicking call—no comparison to the beautiful birdlike call of the bird-voiced tree frog. The tamest is probably the barking tree frog, which in captivity will soon accept hand feeding.

Common tree frog

Three families of salamanders are found only in North

America. Of the 350 species in North and South America, 112 occur in the United States.

Salamanders are more secretive than frogs and often are mistaken for lizards. Long and slender and with a variety of color and patterns, they are mostly six to eight inches long, though the giant salamander of New York, Alabama and Georgia can reach a length of two feet. The mudpuppy is probably the most widespread and common and no doubt the best known. It is large— eight to sixteen inches long—and a gray to brown color. In the spring the female lays about 100 eggs, which hatch about seven weeks later. The tiger salamander is also common and is often seen on a wet night. In some areas the fertility of salamanders is affected by acid rain.

Mudpuppy

Newts are much smaller, and there are six species in the United States. Their skin is not so smooth and slimy as salamanders'; it is more like the skin of the toad. No doubt this is because most species live on land for most of their time and return to ponds only to breed. They vary in size between two and seven inches long and resemble a cross between a lizard and a salamander. They, too, feed on insects and have enormous appetites. The eggs are laid and attached to vegetation or the underside of rocks. Some species lay eggs one at a time, while others lay clusters of ten or twelve.

Handling Hazards
The only problem is with the toad. Its irritant secretions will not normally penetrate the skin, but they could hurt if you have an open cut on your hand. The poison of the giant toad is particularly powerful and has occasionally killed a dog or cat which has bitten one.

Capture
As for reptiles.

Transportation
Transportation should be in moist surroundings—i.e., damp moss or tissues in a wooden box.

Initial Care
Keep quiet and moist in an old aquarium in which there is some water and a dry standing area.

Food
Slugs and insects.

Symptoms, Diagnosis and Treatment
The authors have only experience of injuries, and they usually heal fairly well. If a limb of a newt gets damaged, it can regrow from a stump. Some salamanders can shed their tails where they are gripped by predators, thus effecting an escape while the predator feeds on the tail end. The tail soon regrows.

Release
Release should be in the place or area where the animal was found.

20

Fish

Fish are also cold-blooded and have an advantage over reptiles and amphibia in that the temperature and often the composition of their environment vary only within narrow limits. They have become so specialized that fresh-water fish will not, as a rule, live in the sea, nor sea fish in rivers and lakes. There are exceptions, and the salmon is the most obvious. It does spend most of its life in the sea, however, when it enters rivers to mate and spawn, its physiology changes drastically and eventually it dies there.

Because the body fluids of river fish are saltier than river water, there is a tendency for water to be absorbed; therefore, the fish does not drink, and it passes urine. The body fluids of a sea fish are less salty than the sea, and there is a tendency for it to lose fluids; therefore, it drinks, and it does not pass urine.

Like all animals, fish require oxygen and must eliminate carbon dioxide, a produce of metabolism. This is accomplished by the gills, which act as a sort of lung. The oxygen in the water is partly dissolved from the air and partly given off by plants in the daytime, when photosynthesis occurs. The colder the water, the more oxygen is present there. And of course, the greater the surface exposed to the air, as in rapids or in a waterfall, the more oxygen is dissolved. So slow-moving rivers or still lakes in summer will provide less oxygen for fish, and there will be even less should there be black, smelly, decaying matter along the banks and bottom—all of which means fewer fish.

Another advantage of water is that it supports the body weight, so, as one might expect, it is home to the largest animal that has ever lived—a mammal, not a fish: the blue whale. The largest fish is the whale shark, which is not a whale and certainly does not act like a shark, for it is a vegetarian. It grows to fifty feet in length.

As fish increase in size year by year, their scales get bigger rather than become more numerous. And because growth is faster in the summer when food is more plentiful, each scale develops a ring for each year, rather like trees. It is possible to age the fish by counting these rings.

Some species of fish are loners, and others, such as cod, live together in aggregations. Still other species form schools where each individual is correctly spaced from the next for swimming. And finally there are pods where the fish are so close as to be in actual physical contact.

Schooling is most common in pelagic (deep-sea) fish, such as the herring. A big school behaves almost as if it were a single organism, and the fish are usually of uniform size like "cells." These schools are prone to circle, playing Follow the Leader, especially in confined spaces. Sound may play a major part in keeping the school together, for not only do most fish have good "hearing," but many make sounds, some of such low frequency as to be inaudible to the human ear. Scientists have recorded and played back these sounds and been able to make the school change direction. Watching a school gives one the impression that there is some central control mechanism, so perfectly do the individuals act together. It could be, however, that the human eye is unable to detect the minute movements of each individual, beginning with the change of direction of one fish, which then becomes the new leader.

Although fish are sensitive to sound, they cannot hear in our sense of the word, for they have no ears as we know them. They have neither eardrum nor inner ear structure which makes up the hearing apparatus in mammals. It seems likely that they sense sound waves, using their gas bladder as a resonator. Certainly a fish can detect a footstep on the riverbank and the beat of a ship's propeller.

Fish have not only most of the senses to which we are accustomed but a further sense that records subtle changes in the flow of water around them. It is unique to fish and consists of a canal system, called the lateral line, that contains nerve organs connected to the brain. Scientists have yet to discover all the secrets of this "sixth

Trout

sense," but it seems to record disturbances in the water around the fish and changes in the direction of flow, for cutting the nerves to the brain from these organs interrupts this ability. It is obviously valuable in keeping fish in schools at the correct distance from each other and in telling fish where obstacles lie in murky water.

The sense of touch is carried by small nerve organs scattered over the skin, and they are particularly abundant around the head and lips. Few species have taste buds, but the sense of smell is highly developed in most fish, and they have the equivalent of our nostrils. Although these appear small, the cavity behind is lined with folded walls to provide a maximum surface for sensation. In most fish the sense of smell is so acute that they seem to use it rather than sight in seeking out their food. Sharks, for example, can smell blood from a great distance. It is thought to be this sense that guides the salmon thousands of miles back to the river of its birth to breed.

Eels are also said to use this sense of smell for navigation throughout their dramatic migratory/breeding cycle. So complex is this cycle that no one ever recorded a fresh-water eel with mature sex organs until the end of the eighteenth century. In 1896 two Italian scientists found larval eels in the Strait of Messina. Then at the beginning of this century Danish scientists found that eels spawn in the Sargasso Sea at depths of about 200 fathoms and the larvae drift with the Gulf Stream, taking approximately two years to reach the coasts of Europe, by which time they are elvers about three inches long. They migrate up rivers in swarms and grow to yellow eels. Finally one summer they make for the sea, lose their digestive system, become silver in color and migrate back to where they were born to breed and die.

The eyes of fish function in much the same way as those of terrestrial mammals. There are, of course, some differences—for example, fish that feed on flies above the water have to compensate for refraction of light. There is also less light available in water, so not only do fish get along without eyelids, but they can manage with little or no contraction of the iris. Most of the time fish need see only a short distance ahead, and vision is restricted, at best, to about 100 feet. Since the lens is almost of the same density as water to allow for refraction, it has to be almost spherical. Because the eyes are set on either side of the head, vision is monocular, and although this makes it difficult to judge distances, it has the advantage of allowing the fish to see in more than one direction at a time. It is not known to what degree fish can see color, although it is generally accepted that all fish, except for sharks, have some color vision.

The total fish harvest worldwide has been climbing steadily peaking at 70 million tons in 1970 and declining in the three years following. Experts believe it cannot be greater than 100 million tons without upsetting the reproductive cycles. Most of this vast quantity of fish is caught in nets, hauled out of the sea and allowed to die on the decks and in the holds. Is it cruel? Do fish suffer? Can they feel pain?

This problem was investigated in England by a panel of experts under the chairmanship of Lord Cranbrook, himself a biologist, and their report was published in May 1980 after three years' work. They concluded that although there may be people who will argue that it cannot be proved beyond question that any vertebrate other than a human being feels pain, if any animals feel pain, then the evidence suggests that all vertebrates (including fish) experience similar sensation to a greater or lesser degree.

Twenty-nine years earlier an English government committee on cruelty to wild animals said that pain was of the utmost value to animals in teaching the avoidance of what is harmful to it. "Pain," the committee said, "is therefore a sensation of clear-out biological usefulness. . . ." But of course, it was talking of what occurs in the wild, not the pain and suffering inflicted by the human being's sophisticated methods—to which animals are not biologically adapted.

Recent research has elucidated the function of nerve receptors and the biochemical means of transmitting pain sensation. A polypeptide known as substance P and a naturally occuring pain-killing substance which chemically resembles morphine and is called enkephalin are important in the transmission of pain. Fish possess these chemicals at much the same levels as mammals; therefore, when a fish is hooked, it is kinder to kill it quickly before attempting to remove the hook.

Fish are susceptible to a number of diseases, and eight of these—most of them virus diseases which are not responsive to antibiotics—are notifiable to the authorities. So even if you find and diagnose a diseased fish, there is little that can be done apart from killing it as painlessly as possible (see Appendix B). It is also important to remember that apart from the fact that handling fish out of water with bare hands or in a cloth may be very painful, handling damages the skin, causing osmotic breakdown and rendering it more susceptible to infection. The stress may also precipitate disease. Skin infection, often fungal, is not uncommon after handling in a fishing competition, for example, especially if the fish are kept in a crowded net in a backwater where the flow of water is slow.

Information on the diseases of captive fish in fish farms or in tropical tanks is accumulating fast, but it does not come within the scope of this book.

Fish can be easily poisoned. Nitrates from untreated sewage, chemical pollutants from factories and runoff water from agricultural land treated with pesticides or herbicides—all take their toll on lake and river fish. The sea is large enough to dilute most poisons, but occasionally disasters can occur. One of the worst is the red tide, which can occur all over the world. When conditions are right, a tiny dinoflagellate—a plankton—rapidly multiplies and gives off a toxin which is poisonous to many species. In 1957 a Soviet research vessel reported sighting millions of dead fish floating in the Arabian Sea, covering an area of 80,000 square miles.

Fish have been found to have sublethal amounts of poisonous substances in their bodies without showing any symptoms of poisoning. But they are dangerous to eat, and poisonings of human beings have occurred, the most widely reported being of Japanese fisherfolk.

21

Insects

Insects cannot be ignored, and one good reason is the sheer number and diversity of them. One acre of forest soil probably contains 425 million insects, and the total population of insects on earth is estimated at about 10 billion billion. The total weight of all the insects on earth is about twelve times that of the human population. Their breeding rate is also astounding because they can produce dozens of generations per season. For example, the cabbage aphid will normally produce 40 young per female and will have sixteen generations in a season. If all remained alive and bred, a single aphid at the beginning of the season would account for a total population of 1,560,000,000,000,000,000,000,000 by the end!

It is estimated that there are about 5 million species of living creatures on earth, though only half have so far been identified, and 800,000 of these are insects. At least 100,000 are to be found in the United States.

Stag beetle (male)

What do we understand by the word *insect*? In biological terms insects all belong to the one phylum, or major subsection of the animal kingdom, called Arthropoda, which means possessing jointed limbs and an external skeleton. Instead of having skeletons surrounded by flesh, they have hard, strengthened outer skeletons with the flesh or muscles and blood vessels and organs inside. Insects, in the biological sense, that is, are the only arthropods to possess wings, and none of them has more than six true legs in the adult stage. The juvenile forms such as caterpillars, however, frequently have many more.

In this chapter we will use the word *insect* in its more colloquial sense to mean all those creepy crawlies that are obviously not fish, amphibia or reptiles.

Insects' respiratory systems are not like ours. Their

circulation carries food material to tissues and takes away waste products. It does not transport oxygen as the blood of mammals does. Insects breathe through tubes called spicules, and it is for this reason that an aerosol of fine oil droplets is lethal to them, for they block these tiny tubes and the insect dies of suffocation. The majority of insects live solitary, independent lives, intent on fulfilling their own needs and continuing their species. Many have complicated life cycles that seem to demand a highly developed brain. But the behavior is predetermined by genes. Some insects—for example, bees, wasps and ants—are truly social and behave almost as if they had no lives of their own but were simply cells of the body which is the nest or hive.

Some insects are essentially parasitic on mammals and bite their host to obtain blood. Examples of this group are mosquitoes, midges, fleas, lice, bedbugs and horse flies. Quite a number of insects have stings, which they will use for protection or defense. Others such as the ichneumon wasps use their stings to paralyze their prey.

Communication between insects is very important for most species and is accomplished in several ways. Moths use scent, called pheromone by scientists, which is emitted by the female and can be detected over considerable distances and at a very low dilution by males.

Common grasshopper

Other species—grasshoppers and crickets, for example—use sound as a means of bringing the two sexes together. Grasshoppers do this by rubbing the upper part of their long hindlegs against a ridge on their wing covers, and crickets, by rubbing one wing cover against the other. Of course, many insect sounds are involuntary, being caused by their wingbeats.

Honeybees communicate with each other by performing little dances in the hive. This tells the onlookers that a source of food has been found, *where* it is and how far from the hive—a truly remarkable piece of communication.

Far from advising how to get rid of wasps and bees, we should like to emphasize that they are valuable assets to the gardener as well as interesting to watch. Wasps help keep pest species under control, and bees pollinate our fruit and vegetables.

Of course, both can sting, but only if disturbed. Wasps may attack if you stand too near the nest or if

Wasp

you gesticulate wildly when one comes near. Left alone, it will go away.

Bees have barbed stings which usually remain in the flesh. This means the sting is torn out of the bee's body, and the bee dies. Thus it will not sting unless there is good reason.

Honeybees are not, of course, native to the United States. They originate from the hotter climate of Asia, so hibernate in the winter. In summer they increase by swarming—a queen with many thousands of bees will leave the hive and set up house elsewhere. Though it is terrifying to be near, they rarely sting at this time, for they are far too busy. Having left the hive, they alight on a nearby branch or some other protrusion in a seething mass weighing several pounds, while scouts are sent out to find a new home. This is not an easy task for a forest-dwelling tropical insect, and it needs the help of a friendly human beekeeper. To keep the swarm from moving until he or she arrives, it is useful to simulate rain (without drenching them) and thunder (by banging saucepans etc.).

A great many insects are active at night, and the most obvious are the moths. In fact, most of the U.S. species are nocturnal. However, they do need small amounts of light to become active, and perhaps this explains why moths are so attracted, apparently compulsorily, to artificial light.

Some species, the glowworm and fireflies, make their own light, and they make dazzling displays. I have spent a fascinating evening by a hippo pool watching a dazzling display of fireflies, the light from these tiny creatures pulsating on and off as they wheeled to and fro. The light is produced by a chemical reaction which takes place when oxygen is directed to a substance called luciferin in the presence of certain enzyme. Even more extraordinary, in the case of the glowworm, is that at the back of this chemical is a layer of reflecting crystals which acts like a mirror to reflect all the light that is produced toward the outside. Apparently all the energy is converted into light with no wastage, a lesson which people should learn in these days of energy crisis.

Not content with sharing the wild areas with us, insects invade our gardens and houses. Perhaps the most common and best-known insect that invades our houses is the housefly (*Musca domestica*). The common housefly, however, is actually far less common than it was fifty years ago, partly because of the widespread use of insecticide and also because of improved sanitation and a decline in the use of the horse—for the housefly breeds in dung and filth. For this reason and also the fact that it regurgitates fluid onto whatever food it wants to ingest, it is a dangerous carrier of germs.

Not so the cockroach, one of fifty-five species occurring in the United States, which is a confirmed scavenger and is found wherever there is food material in plentiful supply. It probably does a useful job in clearing up food debris, it certainly presents no threat to human beings, and its presence does *not* denote a dirty house. Perhaps it is so feared and hated because it is nocturnal; when you've got up to get a drink of water, it *can* be a little spine-chilling to see cockroaches scurrying away in the middle of the night. I must have done this once in Teheran—more than half-asleep—for when I came down to the kitchen the next morning, I found my footsteps across the floor to the sink outlined in dead cockroaches!

Common cockroach

Another house dweller, or perhaps one should say kitchen or pantry dweller, is the little silverfish, which can be seen during the day as well as at night. It is a scavenger of food material as well as dead insects. It does us no harm and perhaps a service in clearing up food particles.

Another insect about which most will have heard creepy stories in our youth is the earwig. The cause of the unpopularity, of course, is the generally accepted belief that earwigs will crawl into your ears during the night. Though this is possible, there have been very few reported cases, and certainly an earwig would do absolutely no damage in the ear. It probably would turn round and come out again. Earwigs, like the cockroach and silverfish, are scavengers and help clear away the small food particles that the cook does not see. It may interest women in particular to know that the female earwig is a very good mother, looking after first her eggs until they hatch and then the young, licking them when they hatch and feeding them for a week or two.

Earwig

The furniture beetle, or woodworm, although common out of doors, is often seen in the house. Its natural habitat is dead wood, and it finds tree stumps or sheds just as attractive as floorboards or furniture.

Termites are primitive insects, and more than fifty

species occur in the United States. They live in the soil and eat wood, which is then digested for them by small protozoa living in their gut. Unfortunately they are partial to wood that "man" has fashioned into buildings. And getting into the wood from the soil, they will soon eat it away until the timbers collapse.

Ants prefer to live outside, but who can blame them if they make their nest indoors when there is a plentiful food supply? They are clean creatures that scavenge food particles and cause no harm to human beings unless handled roughly, of course, at which time they will sting. In the garden, where they more commonly make their nest, they help aerate the soil and kill quite a number of species of pests that damage garden plants. They also "farm" and "milk" aphids. They collect aphids and take them alive into their nests, where they "feed" them. Perhaps more commonly, they install the aphids in "cow sheds" around the stems of plants. The aphids suck the juices from the plant and excrete a sweet fluid which the ants then consume. Ants sometimes even collect aphid eggs and store them during the winter. When they hatch in the spring, the ants carry the young aphids out to the plants for "farming." How the ants "know" that the aphid eggs will hatch in the spring and produce the aphids which they want to "farm" is explained by genetics, but how it arose in the first place is unknown.

Perhaps the most disliked and feared of all this group is the house spider, of which there are 30,000 already named and classified. All but a dozen or so are harmless. Spiders are not, biologically speaking, insects. They have eight legs, and insects have only six. All are carnivorous, and the 50,000 or so to be found in each acre of countryside consume many times that number of insects. Because many of their prey are pests, spiders can be called friends, at least of farmers and gardeners. For most species the life span is a year. But there are exceptions such as the tarantula, which can live up to thirty years. Usually thought of as highly dangerous, the bite of the tarantula is about as painful and deadly as a bee sting. In fact, some wasps are far more dangerous than tarantulas.

Some spiders are lethal to children and can make an adult very ill, and a good example is the black widow, recognized by the red hourglass mark on the underside of its pea-sized body. Unfortunately it is widespread through the United States. Its venom, drop by drop, is more potent than that of a rattlesnake. About 1,000 people are bitten each year, and 4 or 5 may die from the bite of the female, the larger of the two sexes.

Some species are as big as dinner plates, and many are as small as pinheads. They have been found in almost every habitat. They are famous for spinning. Many make intricate webs of silk to catch their prey, which they then subdue with a bite from their poisonous fangs. Spiders can race across their webs by walking on the nonsticky radial strands, for only the circular strands are sticky. It is interesting to note that if a spider that normally spins a perfectly proportioned web is given a small amount of "speed" (Dexedrine), the resulting web will be irregular and haphazard. Marijuana- and tranquilizer-treated spiders will spin small webs.

There are many insects that live close to our gardens, where many are disliked, and most are pests. But there is no doubt that the finishing touch to a beautiful flower garden is the sight of a butterfly making its erratic journeys from plant to plant. Alas, with the advent of modern pesticides they are not so common. A few may cause damage (like the large white butterfly to cabbage plants), but most are attracted to buddleias, stinging nettles and wild flowers and cause no damage to vegetables or fruit. To encourage them, a corner of the garden should be allowed to become wild with a wide variety of wild plants, especially those producing nectar. In addition, flowers that are attractive to butterflies can be cultivated; buddleia is the favorite, but lavender, ageratum, honesty, alyssum, petunia, nicotiana and Michaelmas daisies all provide the adult with nectar.

Garden spider

The wings of butterflies and most moths are covered with minute scales which give the color and design, and it is these that rub off on the fingers when the wings are touched. The difference between butterflies and moths, apart from the former's being active in daytime and the latter nocturnal, is that the antennae of butterflies end in small knobs while moths have hairy antennae. Most moths are garden pests in that they can do a considerable amount of damage to fruit and vegetables, for it is not often realized that cutworms are the larvae of a couple of dozen species of moths. As their name implies, they cut into garden and farm crops, feeding mainly at night to avoid predators and resting in the soil during the day.

Caterpillars are mainly the larvae of moths, butterflies and sawflies. Most eat plants from the outside, but some tunnel inside. The cabbage looper is a moth that is common throughout the United States, and the pickleworm, another moth's larva, attacks squash, cucumbers and related plants.

We could mention caterpillars that attack potatoes, tomatoes, celery and many other vegetables, plus, of course, many field crops, adding their share to the $5 to $10 billion worth of annual damage, yet we must hasten to add that of the 100,000 species of insects in the United States, only 600 can be called pests.

We often hear people ask "What use is this or that?" and it is usually dangerous insects, garden pests or just plain nuisances that they are referring to. The insect most often spoken about in these terms is the wasp, for its sting is quite painful. But it is very protective of its young, and if people dare stand in front of the nest, they are inviting trouble. However, as mentioned previously, it does far more good than harm in the garden because it preys upon many insects that gardeners look upon as pests, such as caterpillars.

Aphids, on the other hand, have little to commend them. They are direct competitors to humans and spoil much more garden produce than they consume.

They are also called plant lice, probably because they are small, sucking the plant's sap through a needle-sharp tube. The unfortunate plant's growth is stunted, and it may die. Aphids also spread disease (to plants, not humans) which can be even more disastrous. Aphids breed rapidly into plague numbers unless controlled by predators.

Whiteflies also suck the sap from the undersides of plant leaves and breed rapidly. Leafhoppers, too, are in the same "business" and also spread disease. Some even inject toxin into plants. Though called hoppers, this species does have wings which it opens and uses after leaping into the air on being disturbed.

Speaking of hoppers, there are no fewer than 600 species of grasshopper in the United States. Fortunately damage to crops is caused by only 5 species, but when present in large numbers, they can consume all green vegetation in an area. Apart from loss of the crop, this can lead to soil erosion. There are also many beetle and bug species which damage crops by sucking the plant juices and producing larvae which eat the leaves.

Another hopper, the froghopper, or spittle bug, damages plants when it is in the nymph stage. The nymphs surround themselves with a mass of froth, probably for protection while they feed. They cause damage to many garden plants but are found in largest numbers on alfalfa and other legumes.

Similarly, slugs and snails attack and destroy large amounts of plants that the gardener has been carefully growing. Their only benefit seems to be as food for birds. But slugs and snails prefer rotting material, and the untidy gardener, therefore, will have less to grumble about.

Worms, on the other hand, are very valuable to the gardener. Upward of 1 million per acre may be found in good grasslands, but the numbers in gardens are much lower, probably because of repeated cultivation. Worms come to the surface in the evening, generally warm summer evenings, but rarely leave their burrows completely. They keep their tail ends tucked into the burrow to facilitate a quick retreat while they search around for food or for each other for mating. If you want to see them in the evening in your garden lawn, walk carefully, for worms are highly sensitive to vibration and a heavy footstep will send them immediately back into their burrows. Worms pass a tremendous amount of soil through their bodies, which help break it down into fine material, and their burrows aerate the soil and allow drainage. Dead leaves dragged to the burrows slowly rot away and enrich the soil. Worm casts on a lawn is a sign of a healthy soil. Some gardeners kill them because they find the worms casts unsightly, but all that is needed is a stiff brush to sweep them away. Better to have a healthy lawn and brush away the worm casts than risk poor drainage and the invasion of coarse grasses and weeds.

Another useful garden insect is the delightful-looking little ladybug, which, in fact, is a voracious predator that consumes large quantities of aphids. Ladybugs are also survivors, as the warning red color indicates, for they taste unpleasant and are not eaten by birds. "Look after the ladybug," should be the motto of all gardeners.

Ladybug

English farmers of hop vines recognized their importance many years ago. When burning the dead vines, a necessary process, they worried about killing the ladybugs and used to sing:

> *Ladybug, ladybug, fly away home,*
> *Your house is on fire, your children will burn.*

Dragonfly

But perhaps the most startling attractive insect is the dragonfly. Not all gardeners are fortunate enough to have dragonflies. They are also confirmed predators as both nymphs and adults can catch their prey in flight. Their flight is astounding to watch, as they move swiftly, turn, hover and even fly backward. They are found only near water.

Our enjoyment of the great outdoors is decreased to a certain extent by five main groups of insects: the mosquitoes, midges, black flies, sandflies and Hymenoptera (wasps, bees, ants, etc.). The Hymenoptera are generally only bothersome when disturbed, but the mosquitoes, some species of midges and sandflies are predators on humans in that they are bloodsuckers. Female mosquitoes need a feed of blood before they can lay their eggs, while the male mosquitoes are content to feed on nectar and fruit juices and don't possess the piercing tube found in females. Both larvae and pupae develop in water, and mosquitoes and particularly midges are found most commonly in the moister parts of the United States. Unfortunately they can carry human diseases.

Mosquito

Many readers will remember the timely warning given by Rachel Carson in her revolutionary book called *Silent Spring*, in which she highlighted the extensive use of pesticides and showed how dangerous they were, by extension, to our bird life. Until the last war the pesticides used in agriculture and horticulture were harmless to birds and mammals. Pyrethrum is a naturally occurring product that was fairly effective in the control of many pests, and tar was sprayed on dormant fruit trees to protect them. Only derris was toxic and then only to fish, not to mammals or birds. Then synthetic poisons were discovered, and one of the first was the most effective ever, known by the abbreviation DDT. It is what is called an organochlorine compound and was produced in such vast quantities that traces can be found in the Arctic and Antarctic and in almost all forms of life. It was probably one of the most effective insecticides ever produced, but it had one important draw-back: It was very persistent. Far from being biodegradable, it was taken up and concentrated at each trophic level (in the food chain). This meant that the top predators were consuming, in the bodies of their prey, relatively large amounts of DDT. At first it was thought to be nonpoisonous to mammals and birds, but then it was discovered that when a sufficiently high level in the body was reached, animals showed nervous symptoms, emaciation and diarrhea. Birds with a lower level of pesticide in their bodies developed soft-shelled eggs and low fertility. All the organochlorine compounds — aldrin, Dialdrin and DDT as well as BHC (benzene hexachloride) — are persistent pesticides and where possible should be avoided in the interests of ecology. The red-headed woodpecker and the peregrine falcon were seriously affected and in danger of being exterminated.

Discovered following these were the organophosphorus compounds, which, though just as dangerous, were not quite so persistent in the environment. Mevinphos was one of the first, though other less persistent compounds are highly toxic to humans and protective clothing has to be worn when they are being used.

So if your garden is full of pests that you must get rid of and you do not want to contaminate the environment and endanger birds and mammals, what are you to do? Apart from using safe pesticides, such as pyrethrum or derris or tar oil, there are several ways of preventing infestation with pests before the trouble begins.

Carrot aphid can be largely prevented by firming up the soil when the young carrots are at an early stage of growth and planting shallots or chives between the rows. Flies and aphids are susceptible to nettle manure, which is made by putting a bunch of nettles in a bucket of water, leaving them there for four days, then spraying the fluid onto and around the plants that are being attacked.

Slugs can be killed with Methaldihide. This is sold in most garden shops as slug bait. Slugs are particularly fond of beer, and many gardeners find it useful to sink a jam jar with some beer in it at soil level. The slugs will seek out and drop into the jar. Another method is to put leaves of rhubarb on the ground between your plants; the slugs will seek shelter under them during the night. Early in the morning you simply pick up the leaves and throw them on the compost heap with the slugs attached to the underside.

Rotenone and pyrethrum are effective against caterpillars and will not poison birds that are just as useful in reducing their numbers. The smell of lavender and thyme repels aphids, which also are attacked by ladybugs (see earlier). Scientists find themselves turning more and more to biological control methods: control of a pest species by the encouragement of natural predators or diseases of the pest.

22

Parasites

The word itself makes one uneasy, but it is worth acknowledging that very few wild creatures are free of parasites, whether internal or external. In this chapter we will glance only briefly at their strange world.

Two childhood memories still make Bill shudder. He once picked up a baby swift that had fallen from the nest. It was alive but unconscious. As he cradled it in his hand, two huge (or so they seemed) flattened crablike insects scuttled rapidly onto his hand and up his arm. Bill shook them off in terror. Another time he found, on postmortem, that the intestines of a newly killed chicken were full of large white worms. He remembers wondering how the bird had managed to survive and what it might have suffered.

Some insects are parasitic at only one stage of their development, while others never leave the host, and their harmfulness to the host is largely dependent on their numbers and on the reaction of the host to the parasite. For the parasite to survive successfully, its host has to remain reasonably healthy. However, if the infestation is a large one, disease symptoms and even death can result.

External parasites, or ectoparasites, are generally less likely to cause problems, and birds, for instance, have developed dust bathing, preening and, in certain species, "anting" to keep these parasites under control (see *External or Ectoparasites*). But this equilibrium between host and parasite can be upset by a lowering of the resistence of the birds as a result of weather conditions, food supply and unusual stresses, and the parasites can multiply excessively.

It is perhaps a comforting thought that countless thousands of parasites never achieve their full life cycle. Vast numbers of immature ticks, for example, wait,

Sheep tick (red)

clinging to vegetation, in vain hope that a suitable host will brush past within reach.

Parasites that produce eggs do so by the million to ensure survival; some species reproduce asexually, and others do not and often experience great difficulty in finding a mate.

Many internal parasites absorb food through the surface of their body and have lost their mouthparts and part, at least, of their digestive organs, and almost all internal parasites have complicated life cycles involving intermediate hosts. Many of the species of flukes infecting birds have seven different stages of development: first the egg, then a free-swimming tadpolelike stage, then a cystic stage within the host, then another free-swimming stage and another cystic stage in an intermediate host, which can be anything from mammals and amphibia to jellyfish and even leeches, and finally the mature parasite in the bird. Some species of tapeworm found in foxes use the flea as the intermediate host.

Most internal parasites are host-specific or are restricted to hosts closely resembling each other.

Worms

There are four types of parasitic worm: roundworms, tapeworms and flukes, spiny-headed worms and segmented worms (leeches). Only the last group contains some free-living species. The other three are parasitic, producing millions of eggs with an intermediate stage in another host—for some tapeworms it is the flea, and for some flukes, snails or dragonflies.

The roundworms have a simple cycle within one host. Most species are found in the intestines, but some attack other organs such as the lungs, kidneys and even the heart and the eyes. Many species hatch and develop outside the animal, but some go through the intermediate stage in the blood of their hosts. Postmortems have shown the blood of wild birds to be occasionally teeming with larval worms.

The spiny-headed worms, which have hooks to attach themselves to the host, are mainly parasitic of fish, though a few are found in birds.

External or Ectoparasites

These are not so strongly host-specific as the internal parasitic worms, except perhaps for lice. Even with lice there is one interesting exception in that human lice will feed and breed on pigs, and the pig louse is equally at home on humans.

Ectoparasites are less likely to cause immune reactions, and while flea bites, for instance, can irritate, they may account for birds' "anting." This is quite amusing to watch. As the afflicted birds squat and spread their wings on top of an ants' nest so that they become covered in the insects, others pick up the ants and thrust them under the feathers. Often the abdomens of the ants are burst by the bird's beak, probably releasing the formic acid which may act as a repellent to fleas and lice.

The blood-sucking parasites have developed a type of saliva that prevents blood from clotting and have lost the sensory organs of eyes and ears. These fleas and lice parasitize all vertebrates, and they are more of a nuisance to humans than a hazard except that some can carry disease. They have hard resistant shells and claws adapted for clinging. Fleas are flattened from side to side, and lice from above to below. Fleas have a metamorphosis — i.e., pupa formation in their development — which takes place away from the host. Lice, on the other hand, merely molt to grow. On mammals these parasites live on blood, but on birds the feather louse chews on feathers for food.

Cat flea

Flat flies or louse flies are a highly specialized species. They are large—one-quarter inch long. To the swift they would be as large as a sizable crab to humans, and as many as twenty have been found on a single bird. They are bloodsuckers, have wings, which in some species are vestigial, and seem to "fly" sideways in a hopping manner which most people find rather revolting. They do bite, but this is neither dangerous nor painful. And they produce only one egg at a time, which is hatched inside the insect and is born as a larva, which immediately pupates for the whole winter and hatches in the spring.

Mosquitoes, black flies and midges are common parasitic bloodsuckers which mainly attack mammals, though a few species are specific to birds. They are notorious disease carriers. Wild ducks, for example, are susceptible to a malaria type of parasite which is carried by black flies, and the black fly can also carry a group of worms called *Onchocerca*. Black flies are abundant in late spring and summer in wooded regions of North America.

A parasite that can kill its host is the screwworm fly, which is attracted to wounds on which it lays its numerous eggs. The larvae, when hatched, then begin to devour the host. Control of this fly by the release of millions of sterilized males has been successful in Florida.

Mites are very small—almost microscopic spider-shaped creatures that either live on the skin or burrow into it, causing the disease we call mange in mammals. Red mites are larger and are found in the nests of birds, whose blood they suck from time to time.

Feather mites are not bloodsuckers but feed on skin cells and feathers, as their name suggests.

The lung mite can also affect birds, attacking the bronchial tubes and air sacs.

Ticks are also a species of mite, and they are found on both mammals and birds. They are unpleasant parasites, for their saliva is toxic and one bite can sometimes kill a bird and can cause illness in mammals. Even the eggs contain poisonous substances, and in common with most biting, blood-sucking insects, ticks can transmit diseases. In fact, they are more likely to do so than other biting insects. Rocky Mountain spotted fever is passed by a tick, affecting opossums among others. Woodchucks and other ground squirrels are at grave risk from the Rocky Mountain wood tick, which can cause paralysis and even death.

APPENDICES

Appendix A

Wildlife and the Law

It would be impossible to cover adequately state laws pertaining to wildlife in this book. In any case, it is federal law people are most likely to break in ignorance when trying to help sick and injured wild creatures, so only federal legislation will be dealt with here (and that only briefly).

The purpose of the Migratory Bird Treaty Act is to make the taking, killing or possessing of migratory birds unlawful except under certain circumstances, as authorized by the secretary of the interior. All birds covered are listed but for practical purposes, all but three species found in the United States are migratory. The three (common pigeon, house sparrow and starling) do migrate to some extent but are not protected, being introduced species. The act began as a treaty, first with Great Britain in 1916, with Mexico in 1936 and with Japan in 1972.

Although the act makes the picking up of any listed bird unlawful, for practical purposes the authorities may well show no interest unless the species is endangered. The rarer the bird is, the more interest will be shown. It is, therefore, important to call the local Fish and Wildlife Service (listed under the Department of the Interior) for advice. In each area there are rehabilitation centers for wildlife, several in some states, but their numbers and addresses are not listed. They can be obtained when required from the Fish and Wildlife Service office.*

The act also makes it unlawful to transport listed birds from one state to another or to import a listed bird. No migratory bird may be caught for banding without a permit which should be applied for from the Bird Banding Laboratory Office, Migratory Bird Man-

---

*In addition to government centers, there are, of course many, people doing excellent work in wildlife rehabilitation (see Appendix D).

All lists and appendices referred to are held at all offices of the Fish and Wildlife Service (Department of the Interior).

agement, U.S. Fish and Wildlife Service, Laurel, Maryland 20810.

Because of its particular rarity, there is the Bald Eagle Protection Act which prohibits taking and keeping of the bald eagle. The penalty for breaking this law is greater than for a violation of the Migratory Bird Treaty—namely, a fine of not more than $10,000 and not more than two years in jail.

Subsequent to the Washington Convention (which drew up the Convention on International Trade in Endangered Species of Wild Flora and Fauna) participating countries had to pass their own complying legislation. In the United States the legislation is called the Endangered Species Act of 1973. This act prohibits the trading of endangered species listed in Appendix 1 and requires permits to be issued and the trade controlled of threatened species listed in Appendix 2. The act also prohibits the taking of endangered wildlife but exempts employees of the Fish and Wildlife Service, any other federal land management agency, the National Marine Fisheries Service, or if the wild creature in question is sick, injured or orphaned.

The Lacey Act prohibits the importation of injurious creatures, and though in the main it applies to imports into the United States, it also includes exportation and interstate trade.

Finally, the Marine Mammal Act of 1972 was designed to protect stocks of marine mammals that were in danger of extinction. It prohibits the taking and transporting with certain defined exceptions. Taken overall, this law has given considerable protection to endangered marine mammals, but conservationists are critical of the numbers of dolphins netted and drowned as an incidental to tuna fishing. In 1981 the number involved was said to be about 16,000. There is also concern at the number of bowhead whales, of which there are only a few thousand left, taken by Alaskan Eskimos.

Appendix B

Euthanasia

From the purely technical point of view it is most difficult to describe methods of humanely killing birds and small mammals. A humane death, from the animal's point of view, is instantaneous without any excessive previous stress—such as blowing its head off with a gun while it is quietly resting. However, because the person called up to kill is usually sensitive, kind and reluctant to do so except to relieve suffering, the method must be acceptable and fairly easy to do without any special equipment. The simplest course of action is to take the unfortunate creature to the expert—a veterinarian, the local SPCA or Fish and Wildlife officer. This is not always possible, so we describe below methods which are *practical*, but in no way can we claim that they are anything but unpleasant.

You can kill small birds and mammals by crushing their heads quickly with a stone or your heel, or you can hold them in one hand and swing them sharply down so that the back of the neck and head strikes the edge of a hard ledge. Larger birds can be killed by dislocating the neck. However, this does require a fair amount of strength if the neck is pulled. Alternatively, it can be dislocated or broken with a sharp blow of a stick just behind the head with the bird held so that the head is hanging down. A method for a goose or swan is to lay its head on the ground, put a stick across the neck, stand on it and pull the body sharply upward. This is best carried out after the bird has been stunned with a sharp blow to the head with a stick.

An overdose of the anesthetic ether may be used. However, it is highly inflammable and not easily obtained. To put a small bird to sleep, for example, put two teaspoonfuls on a wad of cotton, and place it beside the bird in a small box just big enough to hold it. The box should be completely airtight until the animal is unconscious, and the operation will take about five to ten minutes.

The neck of a rabbit is dislocated with a sharp blow with the edge of one hand or a heavy short stick, while the animal is held with its head dangling down.

Larger animals should be shot. A twelve-bore shotgun at point-blank range will kill any animal smaller than a deer if placed just above the eyes and pointing down the spine (perpendicular to the skull). The assistance of an experienced marksman should be sought for deer. Use of guns is, of course, restricted to those with licenses to own and use them.

Symptoms of death are: absence of respiration and heartbeat and failure to respond to painful stimuli.

To kill fish, just stun with a blow to the head, and if the blow is strong enough, it will kill. It is best to use a loaded or weighted club that is made for the purpose, and sold by fishing tackle merchants. The blow should be applied to the top of the skull just in front of where the ear might be—but not *too* far forward.

You can kill very small fish by throwing them hard on the ground. Flat fish are harder to kill, and eels are best killed by severing the head from the body after the fish have been stunned with a blow from the club.

Appendix C

Composition of Animal Milks

This list is not comprehensive but gives a representative selection of species appearing in the book.

		% solids	percentage of solids		
			fat	protein	carbo-hydrates
Chapter 8	Short-tailed shrew	21.5	30.2	51.2	14.9
	Cactus mouse	33.1	55.8	39.0	5.1
	California mouse	28.0	67.1	27.5	5.4
	White-footed mouse	28.9	58.8	34.9	6.2
	Canyon mouse	24.7	54.7	37.2	14.8
	Florida mouse	22.8	30.3	63.2	6.5
	Water shrew	35.0	57.1	28.6	0.3
Chapter 9	Fringed myotis	40.5	44.2	29.9	8.4
	Longnose bat	12.1	14.0	36.4	44.6
Chapter 10	Eastern cottontail	33.4	53.6	37.4	3.0
	White-tailed jack rabbit	40.8	34.1	58.1	4.2
Chapter 11	Gray squirrel	39.6	62.5	18.7	9.4
Chapter 12	Ferret	23.5	34.0	25.5	16.2
	Mink	21.2	16.0	35.4	9.4
Chapter 13	Wolf	23.4	41.0	39.3	14.5
	Coyote	24.5	43.7	40.4	12.2
	Arctic fox	29.1	40.5	41.2	18.6
	Red fox	18.2	34.6	34.6	25.3
Chapter 14	Beaver	33.0	60.0	27.3	6.7
	Otter	38.0	63.0	28.9	0.3
	Nutria	43.5	64.1	29.2	1.4
	Porcupine	29.7	44.4	41.8	6.0
Chapter 15	Northern fur seal	65.4	81.5	13.6	0.2
	California sea lion	52.7	69.3	26.2	0.0
	Harp seal	61.6	85.2	9.6	1.5
	Gray seal	67.7	78.6	16.5	3.8
	Hooded seal	50.2	80.5	13.3	0.0
	Northern elephant seal	46.9	62.7	24.9	1.5

	% solids	percentage of solids		
		fat	protein	carbo-hydrates
Chapter 16 Virginia opossum	24.4	28.7	19.7	16.8
Raccoon	16.2	25.9	37.7	29.6
Coati	34.9	42.7	21.2	18.3
Hog-nosed skunk	34.6	31.2	31.2	7.8
Badger	18.6	33.9	38.7	18.8
Chapter 17 White-tailed deer	21.0	38.6	37.1	21.9
Fallow deer	25.3	49.8	25.7	24.1
Mule deer	25.3	43.1	30.0	21.3
Pronghorn	24.9	52.2	27.7	16.1

For this information, we are indebted to Borden, Inc., of Elgin, Illinois, whose milk replacing products for comparison consist as follows:

	% solids	percentage of solids		
		fat	protein	carbo-hydrates
Esbilac (powder)	98.4	44.1	33.2	15.8
Esbilac (liquid)	15.3	44.1	33.2	15.8
KMR	18.2	25.0	42.2	26.1
SPF-LAC	15.2	36.6	33.0	24.8
FOAL-LAC (powder)	94.9	14.4	20.2	56.6

Appendix D

Wildlife Rehabilitation Centers— United States

Wildlife Rehabilitation Council
P.O. Box 3007
Walnut Creek, CA 94598

Lake Tahoe Wildlife Care
P.O. Box 7586
South Lake Tahoe, CA 95731

Alliance for Wildlife
Rehabilitation & Education
P.O. Box 4572
North Hollywood, CA 91607

Wildlife Care Assn.
3615 Auburn Blvd.
Sacramento, CA 95821

North American Wildlife
Center, Inc.
Rt. 1, Box 580
Golden, CO 80401

Tri-State Bird Rescue
P.O. Box 1713
Wilmington, DE 19899

Suncoast Seabird Sanctuary
18328 Gulf Blvd.
Indian Shores, FL 33535

Wildlife Haven
Willowbrook Forest Preserve
525 S. Park Blvd.
Glen Ellyn, IL 60137

Treehouse Wildlife Center
RRI, Box 125 E
Brighton, IL 62012

The Orphan Animal Care
Facility, Inc.
4643 S. Main St.
South Bend, IN 46614

Wild Bird Rehabilitation
Audubon Park Zoo
New Orleans, LA 70178

Chesapeake Bird Sanctuary
10305 King Richard Place
Upper Marlboro, MD 20772

Kalamazoo Nature Center
7000 N. Westnedge
Kalamazoo, MI 49007

Minnesota Wildlife
Assistance Coop.
Rt. 2
St. Cloud, MN 56301

Raptor Research and Rehabilitation
Program
College of Veterinary Medicine
University of Minnesota
St. Paul, MN 55108

Carpenter St. Croix
Valley Nature Center
12805 St. Croix Trail
Hastings, MN 55033

Raptor Rehabilitation and
Propagation Project
Tyson Research Center
Box 193
Eureka, MO 63025

Wildlife Rescue Team
Rt. 1
Walton, NE 68461

The Wild Animal Infirmary
for Nevada
2920 Eagle St.
Carson City, NV 89701

Wild Birds Rehabilitation Research
Center
325 S. First St.
Surf City, NJ 08008

Lifeline for Wildlife, Inc.
RD 104
Ulster Heights Rd.
Ellenville, NY 12428

Hawk Hideaway Rehabilitation Lab
3086 Haskell Rd., RD 2
Cuba, NY 14727

Carolina Raptor Rehabilitation and
Research Center
Department of Biology
University of North Carolina at
Charlotte
Charlotte, NC 28223

Felicidades Wildlife
Foundation, Inc.
P.O. Box 490
Waynesville, NC 28786

Brukner Nature Center
5995 Horseshoe Bend Rd.
Troy, OH 45373

Hawk Mountain Sanctuary
RT 2
Kempton, PA 19529

Wildlife Rescue, Inc.
c/o Austin Nature Center
8411 Adirondack Trail
Austin, TX 78750

Texas Wildlife Rehabilitation
Coalition, Inc.
11506 Chariot
Stafford, TX 77477

Northwoods Wildlife Center
P.O. Box 358
Minocqua, WI 54548

We apologize to any rehabilitators who may be missing from this list. If they would like to be included in any future edition of the book, we will be delighted to hear from them via the publisher. We would also welcome any comments, complimentary or otherwise!

Index

W. J. JORDAN is a world-famous zoologist and veterinarian, formerly chief wildlife officer of the RSPCA (Royal Society for the Prevention of Cruelty to Animals), and now director of the People's Trust for Endangered Species in England.

JOHN HUGHES is warden of the RSPCA Field Unit in England, and is internationally famous for his expertise in saving wildlife casualties, particularly birds trapped in oil slicks.